BRUCE SPRINGSTEEN

BY PATRICK HUMPHRIES

Copyright © 1996 Omnibus Press (A Division of Book Sales Limited)

Edited by Chris Charlesworth
Cover & Book designed by 4i,
Picture research by Nikki Russell

ISBN: 0.7119.5304.X   Order No. OP47802

Exclusive Distributors:
Book Sales Limited, 8/9 Frith Street, London W1V 5TZ, UK.
Music Sales Corporation, 257 Park Avenue South, New York, NY 10010, USA.
Music Sales Pty Limited, 120 Rothschild Avenue, Rosebery, NSW 2018, Australia.

To the Music Trade only:
Music Sales Limited, 8/9, Frith Street, London W1V 5TZ, UK.

Photo credits: All pictures courtesy of LFI and Barry Plummer.

Printed in the United Kingdom by Ebenezer Baylis & Son, Worcester.

A catalogue record for this book is available from the British Library.

W9-AHG-337

OMNIBUS PRESS
LONDON · NEW YORK · SYDNEY

CONTENTS

INTRODUCTION V

GREETINGS FROM ASBURY PARK, N. J. 1
THE WILD, THE INNOCENT & THE E. STREET SHUFFLE 9
BORN TO RUN 17
DARKNESS ON THE EDGE OF TOWN 25
THE RIVER 33
NEBRASKA 45
BORN IN THE U.S.A. 57
BRUCE SPRINGSTEEN & THE E. STREET BAND LIVE/1975-85 67
TUNNEL OF LOVE 75
HUMAN TOUCH & LUCKY TOWN 85
IN CONCERT/MTV PLUGGED 97
GREATEST HITS 101
THE GHOST OF TOM JOAD 109
ODDS & ENDS 117

INDEX 127

INTRODUCTION

They just don't come any better than Bruce Springsteen at his peak. In concert, Springsteen can match the charisma of Elvis, the mystery of Dylan and the commitment of The Clash; even on record, he remains capable of stirring heartfelt emotions and delivering high energy rock'n'roll.

Springsteen's has been one of the most rewarding rock'n'roll careers to follow. He very soon shucked the 'new Dylan' tag which had hung over him during the lifetime of his first two albums. Few people can forget the exhilaration and pure surge of uplifting rock'n'roll energy which poured out of the radio the first time they heard 'Born To Run', and the subsequent album really did seem to match up to all the claims made on Springsteen's behalf. Here was someone capable of marrying the spellbinding lyricism of Bob Dylan with the wall of sound luxury of producer Phil Spector.

'Born To Run''s successor, the bleak 'Darkness On The Edge Of Town', showed that Springsteen was someone who was not necessarily going to play by the rules. The easy option would have been to deliver more of the same, but 'Darkness' was shot through with despair and a sense of alienation, unfortunately though it had precisely that effect on the legion of fans who had flocked to 'Born To Run'.

'The River' again had something for everyone, from the poignant title track to Springsteen's first ever hit single, 'Hungry Heart'. 'Nebraska' two years later was a curve ball, a solo acoustic contemplation of internal grief and political disenchantment, but in its stark simplicity, 'Nebraska' remains arguably Springsteen's most affecting album.

In 1984, everything else paled in the shadow cast by 'Born In The USA', which projected

Springsteen onto a vast new MTV audience. By no means his strongest selection of songs, 'Born In The USA' still turned Springsteen into a household name, with its run of hit singles and high-rotation videos. The 3 CD live set which followed was a stop-gap, and effectively closed a chapter of Springsteen's career.

His next studio album took Springsteen far away from the mainstream audience which had clustered around him with 'Born In The USA'. 1987's 'Tunnel Of Love' consisted largely of further reflections on love and marriage, which as we would soon discover went together like love and… divorce.

It was to be a lengthy five year delay between 'Tunnel Of Love' and the double whammy of 'Lucky Town' and 'Human Touch' in 1992. By then, Springsteen's audience had dissipated, but he had little reason to worry, for a blissfully happy second marriage and parent-hood now took pride of place beside rock'n'roll in the life of Bruce Springsteen.

The release of 'Bruce Springsteen Greatest Hits' early in 1995 was little more than a record company stop-gap, which left long-time fans disillusioned and still hungry-hearted for new material.

Then, out of nowhere, came 'The Ghost Of Tom Joad'. Springsteen-watchers had been anticipating Bruce back with The E. Street Band to pick up where the 'Greatest Hits' tracks had left off. What they got was the bleakest record Springsteen has yet released. A stark, solo companion piece, which made 'Nebraska' sound as bleak as Boyzone.

'The Ghost Of Tom Joad' flew in the face of what was expected, but then, Bruce Springsteen has never played by the rules. It was like he took the late Harry Chapin's words to heart, "I play one night for me, and one night for the other guy". Over the years Springsteen has made one record for himself ('Nebraska', 'Tunnel Of Love', 'The Ghost Of Tom Joad') and one for the fans ('The River', 'Born In The USA' 'Greatest Hits').

'The Ghost Of Tom Joad' is not without fault, but it is a vastly encouraging album for Bruce Springsteen to make, particularly at this time of life and at a stage in his career when he might be expected to take the easy option. After a quarter of a century, 'The Ghost Of Tom Joad' boasts Springsteen's proud deter-mination still to travel the hard road.

There is an engaging directness about Springsteen, and his man-of-the-people image isn't an act. Until his second marriage and the preoccupations of parenthood came along, Springsteen's only commitment was to his work, and that commitment was reflected in a career unmatched in popular music for its intensity and quality.

The best concert I ever saw, was Springsteen live in New York, at Madison Square Garden, November 1980. For over four heart stopping hours, Springsteen just gave everything to that home crowd. He opened with 'Born To Run', and then seemed to play all the best tracks from all his five albums. It was a marathon, take-no-prisoners, all or nothing show. Except that Springsteen did it again, virtually every night for a further 13 months.

I'd known Bruce Springsteen was good, the records had assured me of that. I had never expected him to be that good. So far only a handful of people in the UK had seen Springsteen live, following a pair of shows quickly booked to capitalise on the hype surrounding 'Born To Run' late in 1975. Regrettably, Springsteen himself rated the first of these Hammersmith Odeon shows as among the worst of his entire career.

All we had for those long years away from the UK were the records, and there weren't many of them. Springsteen's absolute determination to make his records the best there were, was the reason for their sparsity. Although, once in the studio, Bruce was a fast and efficient worker, with many of the final versions on record coming from one-take, studio performances. He was also a prolific writer, so there was never any shortage of material for an album – the dozen songs which make up 'Born In The USA', for example, were sifted down from over 100 Springsteen had written.

As a songwriter, Springsteen has never compromised. Until 1992 – aside from a handful of cover versions on the live box set – every track on every Springsteen album was a Bruce Springsteen original. Even prolific peers like Bob Dylan and those who could stack up against Springsteen in the songwriting stakes, such as Elvis Costello and Richard Thompson, have felt the need to collaborate somewhere along the line. It wasn't until 1992's 'Human Touch', widely perceived as his weakest ever album, that Springsteen resorted to collaboration for the first time.

Driven by the desire to make every one of his albums the very best he was capable of, Springsteen went head to head with the legends he'd grown up with. I think one reason why The Beatles are still so fondly remembered is that they distilled all their creative energy into the studio process and onto their records. In comparison, live and on stage, The Rolling Stones probably were "the greatest rock'n'roll band in the world", but their records today sound distinctly tinny, pale souvenirs of those fiery live shows.

What marks Bruce Springsteen as a true rock'n'roll original is his ability to translate the exuberance and intensity of the live concert experience onto record. On disc, Bruce Springsteen is The Beatles and the Stones in one.

For someone who has made his living out of music for nearly a quarter of a century, Springsteen's recorded output makes a small but perfectly formed catalogue. That his reputation remains so high on such a relatively small body of work is as much a testament to the quality of the work as to Springsteen's perfectionism.

Springsteen has released only 11 albums of new material since 1973. In addition to the albums, there have been a number of high quality B-sides, charity records and one-off appearances, which are detailed in the final chapter of this book. But the crucial point

about Bruce Springsteen on record is that he has achieved so much with so little.

Springsteen's dedication to quality and consistency has been the hallmark of his whole career. For three years, between 1975 and 1978, he was legally unable to enter a recording studio, which accounts for some of the delay. But the reason why so little has been officially released by a man who is known to have written – and indeed recorded – so much is mostly to do with his painstaking approach to the recording process.

Springsteen's legendary perfectionism, coupled with his marathon live shows (at one point during the early Eighties, he was pushing four hours and cramming 32 songs into his concerts) has seen him enshrined as the bootleggers' favourite target. For Springsteen fans the attraction of bootlegs is obvious, partly because there is so little product officially available but also because the quality of the mass of material left in the vaults was so high. Like an iceberg, the officially released material is just the tip, with the bulk of his work remaining hidden beneath the surface.

Unlike The Beatles, whose bootlegged legacy includes such dustbin-scrapings as 'Take 7' of George Harrison's guide vocal for 'It's All Too Much', Springsteen is known to have stockpiled a wealth of material over the years – there are still dozens of unreleased songs stretching back to the early Seventies. An effort to beat the bootleggers at their own game resulted in some of the officially unavailable material turning up as bonus tracks on his Greatest Hits collection. With the current vogue for boxing up major artists' careers, Springsteen is an ideal candidate, and a box set of studio material is apparently something both Springsteen and manager Jon Landau have been considering for some years.

But that lies in the future, beyond the reach of this book. This is Bruce Springsteen on record, and where better to begin than at the very beginning…

Christened Bruce Frederick Joseph, Springsteen was born on September 23, 1949, in Freehold, New Jersey, about 15 miles away from Asbury Park, which he would later make world famous.

Bruce was the only son of Douglas & Adele Springsteen. The conflicts between Bruce and his father in later years are well documented on record ('Independence Day', 'My Father's

House', 'Highway Patrolman', the unreleased 'Song To Orphans'). In truth, the arguments probably weren't that different from thousands of others heard around the world at the time (length of the boy's hair, wasn't he ever going to get out of his room, put down the guitar and get a job?) except that Springsteen had the ability to transform them into something universal when he put them into his songs.

As his success burgeoned, Springsteen grew closer to his father, and around the time of 'Born In The USA' in 1984 began to appreciate the pressures which had made Douglas Springsteen into the man he became.

Bruce loved the picture of his father in uniform returning from WWII: "He looked like John Garfield in this great suit, he looked like he was going to eat the photographer's head off. I couldn't ever remember him looking that defiant or proud when I was growing up. I used to wonder what happened to all that pride, how it turned into so much bitterness."

Poorly educated, Springsteen lost his heart to rock'n'roll early on: "Man, when I was nine, I couldn't imagine anyone not wanting to be Elvis Presley." The only son, Bruce spent most of his adolescence in conflict with his father: "When I was growing up there were two things that were unpopular in my house: one was me, the other was my guitar."

Bruce turned in on himself, a solitary child, he sought solace in the sweet music he heard pouring from the radio. Growing up as a teenager in the mid-Sixties, Springsteen got to hear first hand the excitement of The Beatles, Stones, Bob Dylan, The Yardbirds, Them, featuring a young Van Morrison, and Creedence Clearwater Revival.

Despite his lack of formal education, Springsteen was soon able to crystallise the thoughts and dreams, desires and aspirations of every teenager who grew up during those turbulent times. In 1987, he reflected: "If you grew up in my generation, part of the dream of rock'n'roll was eternal youth, the endless Saturday night."

Bruce was no intellectual ("I wasn't brought up in a house where there was a lot of reading and stuff. I was brought up on TV"). Springsteen was keen to learn though, and even if he didn't know the difference between 'Over The Rainbow' and Arthur Rimbaud, his gritty, no-nonsense approach to rock'n'roll helped free it from the rather pretentious intellectual aspirations it had acquired during the Seventies.

Part of the joy of following Springsteen came from watching his development, initially under the hard and fast management of Mike Appel, then through the tutelage of confidante and later manager Jon Landau, as well as with a tightly-knit group of journalists (in particular biographer Dave Marsh), Springsteen was eager to learn. Inevitably, what he learnt eventually wound up on record or was played out in concert – whether it was the books he was beginning to read (the short stories of Flannery O'Connor, a biography of Woody Guthrie) or sounds new to his ears (the mysterious Fifties rock'n'roll of Hank Mizell or the keening country of Hank Williams).

Springsteen certainly paid his dues. His was an apprenticeship forged in the old-fashioned and currently unfashionable academy of rock'n'roll. At no time in his life has Springsteen had any employment other than playing guitar and singing songs. That may explain how he kept shy of some of life's harsher realities, but Springsteen has played his share of the proverbial Monday night gigs to three men and a dog.

He spent much of the mid-Sixties scuffing around the bars of New Jersey, playing gigs for eight years prior to his album début. Springsteen cut his teeth with local Jersey bands The Castiles, with whom he made a demo recording, 'Baby I', cut for $50 at the Brick Mall in May 1966. The Castiles metamorphosed into heavy rockers Earth, who then changed their name to Child in 1968.

It was all go in the zany, happening 1960s: Child changed their name to Steel Mill, which formed the foundation of Springsteen's beloved E.Street Band, drawn from a free-flowing pool of young rock'n'rollers who plied their trade in the clubs and bars of New Jersey during the late Sixties. Late in 1969, Springsteen followed his parents when they moved to California searching for work for Douglas. Steel Mill supported Boz Scaggs and even got round to recording some demos for legendary promoter Bill Graham in San Francisco. Once again, the loose aggregate changed their name, this time to Dr Zoom & The Sonic Boom, but still they failed to make it.

All the while, Springsteen refused to compromise and leave music behind. He is one of rock music's most enthusiastic prisoners.

Bruce couldn't imagine a life without music, even when his life promised nothing but poorly paid gigs and no future: "Rock'n'roll, man, it changed my life. It was... the Voice of America, the real America coming to your home. It was the liberating thing, the way out of the pits. Once I found the guitar, I had the key to the highway."

It was a despairing time, but Springsteen refused to give up hope. Band members testify to Springsteen's commitment, but they were all living on dreams.

Besides himself, the only man to show any faith in Springsteen was a hustling young manager called Mike Appel, whose only previous claim to fame had been writing a hit for The Partridge Family. Appel convinced Bruce that he was the man to steer Springsteen to the toppermost of the poppermost, and so one night early in 1972, on the bonnet of a car in a parking lot – in a flash of naïvety which was to cause him much grief a few years later – Springsteen signed a management deal with Appel.

It was Appel who landed an audition for his protégé with Columbia Records' legendary John Hammond, the man who had nurtured the careers of Benny Goodman, Robert Johnson, Billie Holiday, Aretha Franklin and Bob Dylan. Appel's pitch was "If you're the guy who discovered Dylan for all the right reasons, you won't miss this". (Dave Marsh's account has Appel barking: "You're the guy who discovered Bob Dylan huh? Well, we want to find out if that was just luck or if you really have ears!")

Bruce was happy. He knew Hammond's name from one of the few books he admitted to reading, Anthony Scaduto's biography of Bob Dylan. It was the meeting which sealed Springsteen's future, with Bruce's 15 minute audition turning into a two-hour performance for the clearly delighted record company executive. Hammond envisaged Springsteen as a solo acoustic performer in the style of the young Dylan, but Springsteen had his eyes clearly set on a rock'n'roll future and lost no time re-enlisting his Asbury Park compadres.

Hammond later admitted: "When Bobby came to see me, he was Bobby Zimmerman. He said he was Bob Dylan, he had created all this mystique. Bruce is Bruce Springsteen. And he's much further along, much more developed than Bobby was when he came to me."

Those 1972 Hammond demos threatened to surface in 1994, when they were pressed up by an independent label as 'Prodigal Son', until an injunction from Springsteen, manager Jon Landau and Sony Music blocked their release.

Meanwhile, back in 1972, with a $25,000 advance from Columbia Records in his pocket, Bruce Springsteen finally had the keys to the highway. He was ready to roll…

For True Rockers Only is a quarterly Bruce Springsteen magazine. Details are available from PO Box 35, Cheltenham, Glos., GL50 2YN. Telephone 01242 579425.

Badlands is the shop for Bruce-fanatics. Based in Brian Jones' home town of Cheltenham, Steve & Phil Jump stock all the hard-to-get Springsteen records I mention in the text. They can be contacted on the above telephone number, or faxed on 01242 232353.

GREETINGS FROM ASBURY PARK, N.J.

(COLUMBIA CD32210; RELEASED: JANUARY 1973 [USA], MARCH 1973 [UK])

Hard to believe now, but back at the very beginning, Bruce Springsteen was lumped together with all the other 'new Dylans' of the early Seventies: aspiring singer-songwriters like Steve Goodman, John Prine, Kris Kristofferson and Loudon Wainwright who all laboured under the Dylan comparison.

The singer-songwriter boom in the early part of the decade – spearheaded by the success of James Taylor's 'Sweet Baby James' and Carole King's 'Tapestry' – seemed like a reaction against the increasing complexity, volume and pretentiousness of late Sixties rock music. Dylan was still perceived as a figurehead, but following a succession of weak albums, he had gone to ground, leaving his groundbreaking work from 1963-1966 to cement his reputation in his absence.

Springsteen was a dyed-in-the-wool Dylan fan, inducting the grand old man into the Rock'n'Roll Hall Of Fame in 1988 with the words: "The way that Elvis freed your body, Bob freed your mind. He had the vision and the talent to make a pop song so that it contained the whole world."

One of Springsteen's most endearing characteristics is his genuine enthusiasm for music. Balanced and considered in interview, he transmits a real knowledge of, and enthusiasm for, pop music in all its many forms. In praise of Dylan, he was at his most articulate: "The first time I heard Bob Dylan, I was in the car with my mother and we were listening to 'Like A Rolling Stone' and on came that snare shot that sounded like somebody had kicked open the door to your mind."

But Bruce was no Bob shadow. Even back there at the beginning, Springsteen had covered the waterfront. His influences drew from R&B,

old-time rock'n'roll, soul, Country, folk, jazz, plus an old-fashioned commitment to performance and quality. Bruce had been a fan too long to let down anyone who invested any faith in him.

Wordy and under-produced as 'Greetings From Asbury Park' undoubtedly was, there is still something beguiling in Springsteen's 'coulda bin a contender' album. Figuring he'd only ever get one crack at the title, Bruce poured everything into his début, and while it may not hold a candle to, say, 'Darkness On The Edge Of Town', 'Greetings…' is a valuable snapshot of just where Bruce Springsteen began.

In retrospect, you can see how Bruce Springsteen slotted into early Seventies rock music. The Beatles had split up in 1970, and despite the excellence of 1972's 'Exile On Main Street', the Stones were in a druggy haze of tax exile. If you were looking for a rock icon in 1973 David Bowie was yer man, but not everyone succumbed to Ziggy Stardust. After a thrilling five-year reign as the kings of the live circuit, The Who were running out of steam and Yes' voyages on 'Topographic Oceans' were too fanciful to be taken seriously. Supergroups such as Emerson, Lake & Palmer and Pink Floyd were becoming increasingly

overblown and remote with their stadium spectaculars. Led Zeppelin had taken America by storm but were seen less frequently than UFOs in their homeland.

The teenyboppers were kept happy by T.Rex, Sweet and The Osmonds, but there was a real need for someone who appreciated the traditions of rock'n'roll and could also shine a light on its future. Unwittingly and with a combination of good luck and sheer hard work, Bruce Springsteen fitted the bill.

'Greetings From Asbury Park, NJ' was cut in a week, with familiar names – former James Brown saxophonist Clarence Clemons, organist Danny Federeci, bass player Garry Tallent, drummer Vini 'Mad Dog' Lopez – drawn from the pool of New Jersey musicians with whom Springsteen had worked over the preceding six years.

The evidence is that he tried a tad too hard, choking on the lyrics ("some brimstone baritone anti-cyclone rolling stone…") and letting his versatility overwhelm him – 'Mary Queen Of Arkansas' is unconvincing folk; 'The Angel' deep and meaningless…

A year after its release, talking to long-time supporter Robert Hilburn, Springsteen looked back on 'Greetings From Asbury Park, NJ': "I got a lot of things out on that first album. I let out an incredible amount at once – a million things in each song. They were written in half-hour, 15-minute blasts. I don't know where they came from. A few of them I worked on for a week or so, but most of them were just jets, a real energy situation. I had all that stuff stored up for years, because there was no outlet in the bars I had been playing. No one's listening in a bar, and if they are, you've got a low PA system and they can't hear the words anyway. So that first album was a big outlet."

Many of the album's flaws were due to the cut-price production, manager Mike Appel had little behind the board experience and to save as much of the CBS' advance as they could, Appel and Springsteen plumped for the out of the way 914 Sound Studios.

Early reviews of the album compared Springsteen to Van Morrison and Columbia sold Springsteen on the very wordiness which now sounds so at fault (one ad ran: "This man puts more thoughts, more ideas and images into one song than most people put into an album").

Springsteen's record label was very much aiming to carve out a 'new Dylan' audience; the old one remaining out of the limelight for much of the early Seventies, having left the door wide open for contenders. Richard Williams' review of 'Greetings From Asbury Park' in *Melody Maker* was headlined "A Dylan for the 70s?" ("The comparisons with Dylan will be inevitable, may even hurt him, and there's no denying the influence – but Springsteen is to Dylan as the 1973 Ferrari Berlinetta Boxer is to the 1961 Ferrari 250GT…")

The comparisons with Van Morrison were also made early on, a fact which the notoriously cuddly and lovable Van noted in a rare 1985 interview: "For years people have been saying to me – you know, nudge, nudge – have you heard this guy Springsteen? You should really check him out! I just ignored it. Then four or five months ago, I was in Amsterdam and a friend of mine put on a video. Springsteen came on the video and that was the first time I ever saw him, and he's definitely ripped me off. There's no doubt about that. Not only did Springsteen… I mean, he's even ripped off my movements as well. My Seventies movements, you know what I mean? This stuff" (demonstrates – the mind, she boggle) "I feel pissed off now that I know about it. I'd never seen it before, so I didn't know." The following year, on his 'No Guru, No Method, No Teacher' album, Van included a song 'A Town Called Paradise', the opening lines of which ran: "Copycats ripped off my words, copycats ripped off my songs…"

Neither of the singles lifted from his début album ('Blinded By The Light' and 'Spirit In The Night') troubled the chart statisticians. By the end of 1973, Bruce Springsteen was still very much an acquired taste.

BLINDED BY THE LIGHT

The 'new Dylan' tag was certainly appropriate judging from the opening track, which tipped its hat heavily in the direction of Dylan's 'Subterranean Homesick Blues' from eight years before – which in turn had been inspired by Chuck Berry's 'Too Much Monkey Business'. The song was also Springsteen's first single, but didn't chart in the USA and was never released in the UK. Derivative and wordy as it is, there remains an undeniable drive and refreshing vivacity to 'Blinded By The Light'.

Manfred Mann, who in the Sixties had enjoyed much success with his covers of Dylan songs, thought so too. He covered 'Blinded By The Light' and made it a US No.1 in 1976.

GROWIN' UP

Only when Springsteen exercises some restraint do the songs on his début really come alive. David Bowie recognised the quality of 'Growin' Up' and recorded it for his 1974 album, 'Young Americans', along with 'It's Hard To Be A Saint In The City'; although his 'Growin' Up' failed to surface until 1990 when it appeared as a bonus track on the CD release of 'Pin-Ups'. Any Trouble recorded a cracking version of the song on their 'official bootleg' 'Live At The Venue'. Alvin Stardust did a credible cover too. There is obviously something about the song which is undeniably, effortlessly pure rock'n'roll. 'Growin' Up' is Springsteen at his brashest, his cockiness engaging, and hints at Bruce the literate car mechanic, with the line: "I swear I found the key to the universe in the engine of an old parked car." The song was a firm concert staple well into the Eighties and a 1978 perfor-

mance, recorded at the Roxy, appeared on the three CD live box set – this performance enlivened by an onstage rap from Bruce about growing up in New Jersey, his problems with his dad, the Springsteens' plans for their only son's future ("It's still not too late to go to college") and his plans ("What they didn't understand is that I wanted everything").

MARY QUEEN OF ARKANSAS

Bruce does inscrutable Bob Dylan-type lyrics, and falls flat on his carburettor. Sounding desperately unconvincing and uncomfortable as solo folkie, Bruce covers his discomfort with lyrics as dense and impenetrable as engine oil. You suspect he was told to sound "meaningful" in order to further the Dylan comparisons. Bad career move. The song never featured in concert after 1974.

DOES THIS BUS STOP AT 82ND STREET?

Structurally similar to 'Blinded By The Light', 'Does This Bus…?' is another Springsteen word-fest. Locked around the rich R&B territory of Spanish Harlem, the presence of Joan Fontaine (who played the nameless heroine in Hitchcock's *Rebecca*) is frankly baffling.

LOST IN THE FLOOD

'Lost In The Flood' hints at the epic grandeur Springsteen would achieve some years down the line. Prowling and building to a grandiose and sinister climax, the song was one of the few on his first album which suggested Springsteen had a future beyond that of a Dylan clone. Springsteen's religious upbringing surfaces in bloody detail here, with lurid Catholic imagery rampant – nuns running "through Vatican halls pregnant, pleadin' immaculate conception". But it is the attention to detail in his writing, which suggests later strengths: the pen portrait of the "pure American brother" racing Chevys on Sundays in New Jersey is masterly. Melodically superior though the song is, Springsteen rarely performed 'Lost In The Flood' in concert after 1978.

THE ANGEL

More auto-mechanic imagery, written on auto-pilot; hard to credit that at the the time, Bruce believed it to be his most sophisticated song. Thought never to have been performed live, 'The Angel' is a rambling inconclusive tale of a motorcyclist. Of later interest, the lumpy line "The interstate's chocked with nomadic hordes" would appear, radically rewritten, as "the highway's jammed with broken heroes" on 'Born To Run'. Otherwise, au revoir.

FOR YOU

Uncharacteristic and oddly mature reflection on suicide, 'For You' was a minor hit for Greg Kihn and remains one of the outstanding tracks on Springsteen's début album. Unlike many of the songs here which are taken at a hell for leather speed, with no attempt to pace or to build, 'For You' does both; and while Bruce's lyrics may be syllable suicide, they don't take away from the drama of the narrative.

SPIRIT IN THE NIGHT

Perennial live favourite, helped along by its call and response chorus, 'Spirit In The Night' was one of the songs taken from Springsteen's legendary 1978 shows at the Roxy to appear on his 'Live 1975-85' box set. 'Spirit In The Night' came from that seam of ritualistic camaraderie which Springsteen mined so heavily on his first three albums. Manfred Mann's Earth Band reached No.40 in the US charts with the song in 1977 – the Mann man also covered 'For You' to round off a trio of covers from Bruce's début album.

IT'S HARD TO BE A SAINT IN THE CITY

'It's Hard To Be A Saint In The City' has that street-suss sound which Springsteen later honed and perfected. Here is all the cockiness and arrogance that the whole album needed if it was to succeed. 'It's Hard To Be A Saint In The City' was the first song Springsteen played for John Hammond at his CBS audition, and you can hear what captivated the esteemed A&R man. Here is the language of the street, riffing along to a compulsive, low-key rock'n'roll beat. The religious imagery was also to be found on another song Springsteen performed for a delighted Hammond, the still unreleased 'If I Was The Priest'. But more assuredly, Springsteen casts himself as Marlon Brando and Casanova. The boy was learning fast.

BRUCE SPRINGSTEEN THE WILD, THE
INNOCENT & THE E STREET SHUFFLE

THE WILD, THE INNOCENT & THE E. STREET SHUFFLE

(COLUMBIA CDCBS 32363; RELEASED: SEPTEMBER 1973 [USA], FEBRUARY 1974 [UK])

With the first album selling only to immediate family – the first 12 months' sales of 'Greetings From Asbury Park' barely totalled more than 25,000 – Springsteen's label pushed their new signing out on tour in an attempt to drum up some interest. During 1973 and to the end of 1974, Springsteen consolidated his live reputation, and dutifully did the opening act bit. But slots supporting Bob Marley & The Wailers, Chicago, Chuck Berry, Black Oak Arkansas, Bonnie Raitt and Dr John did not help. Prior to the release of 'Born To Run', Springsteen even opened for songbird Anne Murray at a massive show in New York's Central Park, though it should be noted that most of the audience went home after Bruce's set.

Yet nothing seemed to help, great reviews weren't shifting records. The boy was all set to go belly-up.

In one of the first pieces on Springsteen to be published in the UK, *Zigzag*'s Jerry Gilbert remembers interviewing Bruce pre-'Born To Run': "We're at the lowest we've ever been right now. It means that if we don't play every week of the year, then we don't have money. Right now we've just come off the road and the guys are getting thrown out of their houses.

"Hopefully I'll be getting some money from Columbia, and maybe with David Bowie doing some of the songs that'll be good. But that's the only problem right now, it's sort of a shame, I'd just like to be a little more secure, that's all."

Then on May 9, 1974, opening for Bonnie Raitt in Cambridge, Massachusetts, everything fell into place. It was the night Springsteen had chosen to première a new song – 'Born To Run' – by chance he also found himself chatting to an impressed journalist. It was the resulting piece by ex-*Rolling Stone* staffer and occasional record producer Jon Landau, which forever altered Springsteen's future.

Landau's feature ran in Boston's *Real Paper* late in May 1974. It was part reflective ("Today I listen to music with a certain sense of detachment. I'm a professional and I make my living commenting on it... I'm twenty-seven today, feeling old, listening to my records and remembering that things were different a decade ago... On a night when I needed to feel young, he made me feel like I was hearing music for the first time"); part queasy hype ("He is a rock'n'roll punk, a Latin street poet, a ballet dancer, an actor, a joker..."). But all the world remembered was one line: "I saw rock 'n'roll future, and its name is Bruce Springsteen". Landau's quote remains perhaps the best known piece of rock'n'roll criticism ever penned. It was a line which Columbia thankfully jumped on, and built an entire campaign around.

To his chagrin, it was the line which salvaged Bruce Springsteen's career. It didn't harm Jon Landau either. From that chance encounter outside the Harvard Square Theater, Landau went on to co-produce every

subsequent Springsteen album (apart from the home-grown 'Nebraska') and from 1977 onwards he was Springsteen's manager.

Even before Landau's piece ran, Springsteen's second album, 'The Wild, The Innocent & The E.Street Shuffle' had at least arrested the decline in Springsteen's fortunes. His second album was less frenetic and a much more considered work, which suggested that there really was something special in this brightest of the new Bobs.

For years, 'Rosalita' was Springsteen's show-stopper, a pounding rocker which still throbs in all the right places. But the true strengths of the second album became apparent on the slower, more reflective songs: 'Sandy' was a poignant memory of Springsteen's adolescence, whiled away around the crumbling seaside resorts of New Jersey; 'Wild Billy's Circus Story' was a curious acoustic account of circus life; 'Incident On 57th Street' was a bona-fide rock'n'roll classic, marked by its slow, stately progress.

Despite poor sales, Springsteen was growing in confidence. In performance, his following was increasing all the time, while his band forged their reputation as a hot draw and all the while he was honing his songwriting skills. But Springsteen still needed that killer album to consolidate his burgeoning live reputation. 'The Wild, The Innocent & The E.Street Shuffle' wasn't it, but it was a step in the right direction. It was very much a transitional work, Springsteen having got the clumsiness out of his system on his début.

People were beginning to sit up and take notice. In his review of The Wild, The Innocent & The E.Street Shuffle, Ken Emerson wrote in *Rolling Stone*: "'Greetings from Asbury Park', Bruce Springsteen's uproarious début album sounded like 'Subterranean Homesick Blues' played at 78, a typical five-minute track bursting with more words than this review... 'The Wild, The Innocent & The E.Street Shuffle' takes itself more seriously. The songs are longer, more ambitious, and more romantic; and yet,

wonderfully, they lose little of 'Greetings" rol-licking rush. Having released two fine albums in less than a year, Springsteen is obviously a considerable new talent."

Only seven tracks made it onto Springsteen's second album. Among those recorded but not included, were the haunting 'Zero & Blind Terry', 'Hey Santa Anna' and the boisterous 'Seaside Bar Song'. Other titles considered for the album were 'Angel's Blues', 'Calvin Jones & The Thirteenth Apostle', 'Casper', 'Thundercrack', 'Ballad Of The Self-Loading Pistol' and 'The Fever'.

Looking back eight years on, Springsteen recalled: "On the second album, I started slowly to find out who I am and where I wanted to be. It was like coming out of the shadow of various influences and trying to be yourself."

THE E.STREET SHUFFLE

'The E.Street Shuffle' was a good, emphatic opener, even if it does sound a mite thin on CD today. The song is a testament to Springsteen's brassy buddy, long-time saxophonist Clarence Clemons, with its punchy brass-led, soul riffs. This was the song which helped to name Springsteen's band for the next decade. Pianist David Sancious' mother lived on E.Street, Belmar, New Jersey, which was where the name came from. Bette Midler later recorded the song.

4TH OF JULY, ASBURY PARK (SANDY)

Undeniably Springsteen's first truly great song on record. 'Sandy' is an atmospheric tale of life and love under the boardwalk. Springsteen pours his heart and soul into 'Sandy', his voice too injecting every last ounce of passion into the song. Made all the more poignant by Danny Federici's accordion, 'Sandy' is a bitter-sweet memory of Bruce growing up along the Jersey shore, eloquently and graphically evoking the out-of-season beach resort, crammed with as many memories as there are grains of sand along the beach. The Hollies made chart history when they became the first act to chart with a cover of a Springsteen song – their prettified version of 'Sandy' reaching No. 85 in America in 1975. The version of 'Sandy' which Springsteen included on his 'Live 1975-85' box set features an extended third verse, introducing angels riding "down from heaven on their Harleys."

KITTY'S BACK

Fairly anonymous mid-paced rocker. Opening with some scorching Springsteen guitar, the song soon gets bogged down in a quagmire of riffs. Close to the sound and structures of his first album, Bruce plays it cocky. The brass get it off their chest, and there is the first clear indication of the influence pianist and organist David Sancious' jazz roots were to have on this down-the-line rocker.

WILD BILLY'S CIRCUS STORY

One of Springsteen's most uncharacteristic songs. As with the previous album's 'Mary Queen Of Arkansas', you sense Springsteen was having "versatility" chucked at him. Rock'n'roll has had close links with circus life (The Everly Brothers' 'Ferris Wheel', The Beatles' 'Being For The Benefit Of Mr Kite', Richard Thompson's 'Wall Of Death') and

Bruce does his best with this quirky contribution. It sounds like he's having fun with it, especially when bassist Garry Tallent's tuba gets to impersonate an elephant; Tom Waits even singled the song out as one of his favourite Springsteen compositions. Significantly, in view of his 1982 album, the song ends with Springsteen drawing attention to the circus' next destination: "All aboard, Nebraska's our next stop".

INCIDENT ON 57TH STREET

The real indication that there was more here than just bluster came on the taut 'Incident On 57th Street'. Starting slow and building, Springsteen had not sung with such fervour before, he sounded like he knew these people, not like he'd drawn them up from his imagination. This is the moment when Springsteen the writer came into his own. He formed characters from jotted-down observations and gave them idiosyncrasies of their own to create a convincing whole and then dropped them into familiar real-life locations. You can hear where Mark Knopfler got the structure for

'Romeo & Juliet' from. 'Incident On 57th Street' was, along with 'Sandy', the sound of Springsteen in control. All the elements come together here, to make a song which is more than the sum of its parts: a passionate vocal, searing guitar, Spector-ish backing vocals, far-away saxophones… all combine to present a fire-escape view of street life. An impressive 10-minute version of the song turned up as the B-side of the 1986 single 'War'. 'Incident On 57th Street' was *West Side Story* re-writ for the rock'n'roll era.

ROSALITA (COME OUT TONIGHT)

For many years, Rosalita was probably Springsteen's best loved song in the UK. This was largely thanks to a performance, shot in Phoenix, Arizona in July 1978, which for a long time, was the only glimpse of Springsteen available to his British fans (usually courtesy of endless re-viewings on *The Old Grey Whistle Test*). Similar to 'Blinded By The Light' in its mythologising of New Jersey, 'Rosalita' nevertheless has a deftness and lightness which Springsteen's cumbersome

earlier efforts lacked. There is a freneticism and buoyancy here. Live, it has remained a firm staple of Springsteen in concert, and indeed was the concert-closer at every Springsteen show for 11 years, from 1973 to 1984. The place never fails to erupt as he sings "The record company… paid me a big advance". 'Rosalita' offers room for Clemons' saxophone to roam, for Bruce to leap around the stage and for capacity crowds to shed years and go out on a teenage rampage.

NEW YORK CITY SERENADE

The near 10-minute 'New York City Serenade' was Springsteen's ill-conceived concession to jazz. It probably came under his heading of "sophisticated" and was influenced by David Sancious, though Sancious who had also studied classical piano, was just as likely to drop in a snatch of Mozart as a jazz phrase. The song had begun life as 'Vibes Man', which Springsteen had performed at the John Hammond audition in 1972. Clemons' sax plays out, but the song – the longest studio piece Springsteen has ever recorded – just doesn't hang together.

BORN TO RUN

(COLUMBIA CDCBS 80959; RELEASED: AUGUST 1975 [USA], OCTOBER 1975 [UK])

It was the record nobody wanted. Columbia weren't exactly rubbing their hands at the prospect of a third album from Bruce Springsteen, the label was concentrating on new releases from their established and consistently best-selling acts like Chicago, Barbra Streisand and Paul Simon. Springsteen's previous two albums and two singles ('Blinded By The Light', 'Spirit In The Night') had sold less than 90,000 copies in total. This third album really would be make or break.

Springsteen himself knew how crucial his third album was, if he didn't come up to snuff, he was off the label. That knowledge weighed heavily and he was reluctant to let the third album out of his grasp.

Two years into his professional career, Springsteen was still dogged by the "new Dylan" tag. Although he had built quite a reputation as a unique live performer, with shows stretching from 75 minute showcases to two-hour spectaculars, Bruce knew that everything rested on the success of his third album. Fans wanted something more representative of those breathtaking live shows than the flimsy-sounding albums currently available.

The only thing Springsteen had going for him when the time came to begin his third album, was a new song called 'Born To Run' which had been going down well in concert.

In August 1974, along with manager Mike Appel, Springsteen repaired to 914 Sound Studios, at Blauvelt in New York State, where his first two albums had been recorded. The fruit of the 914 sessions were four separate mixes (some including strings and a female chorus) of one track only, 'Born To Run'. But Springsteen was unhappy with the technical quality of the studio and on the advice of Jon

Landau, who was already on his way to becoming an integral member of the Springsteen team, production moved to New York's Record Plant.

Springsteen seemed to have found a soul mate in the journalist, but the presence of Landau only widened the gulf between the artist and his manager Mike Appel. Ironically, in view of the differences which developed, the finished, world-famous version of 'Born To Run' was a joint production between Springsteen and Appel.

Springsteen had a clear vision of how he wanted the finished 'Born To Run' album to sound – like Roy Orbison singing the lyrics of Bob Dylan to a Phil Spector production. To his credit, he came within a whisker, but getting there was a nightmare. "The album became a monster," reflected Springsteen later. "It just ate up everyone's life."

Band personnel were a problem too. E.Street Band drummer, Vini 'Mad Dog' Lopez had just been fired and his replacement Ernest 'Boom' Carter stayed only long enough to play on the album's title track, while pianist David Sancious quit to pursue a solo career. Feeling that his manager wasn't

protecting him sufficiently from the label's indifference, Springsteen confided more and more in Landau. Gradually, the axis shifted, and Landau found his opinions sought on the actual recording of the album.

Landau did have some experience in record production, with albums by the MC5, James Taylor's younger brother Livingstone and J. Geils Band to his credit. Mike Appel was, predictably, less than happy with the situation: "I believe Landau had it in his mind all along, once he saw Springsteen and declared him rock and roll's future, to produce Bruce and eventually take over his management... The best I can say about Landau as a producer, prior to working with Bruce, was that he was a heck of a critic." The battle for the soul and future of Bruce Springsteen raged in the studio.

Mike Appel recalled the stresses and strains in Marc Eliot's under-rated Springsteen biography *Down Thunder Road*: "Bruce had lost his direction, his energy, and to some extent his confidence. We'd been at it now for a year, deep in debt to the label, no enthusiasm up at CBS for us, continual personnel shifts, so when there were technical breakdowns, it was easy to start shifting the blame as to why things weren't happening."

It was only when DJs started playing leaked copies of the 'Born To Run' single that Columbia began to get behind the album. With costs rising above $50,000, and sessions which had begun in the summer of 1974, the recording of the album now stretched into 1975. Springsteen had the songs, some of his best ('Born To Run', 'Thunder Road', 'Backstreets', 'Jungleland'), but the *sound* was eluding him. The sessions just dragged on and on.

Springsteen the perfectionist fell asleep at mixing sessions, he chucked one finished master out of a hotel window because it hadn't captured the sound he was chasing. He knew he was taking a gamble, but he knew everything rested on this third roll of the dice. Pressure was on to get the album finished, but Landau remembers being impressed by Springsteen's determination as the record company applied further pressure to rush release 'Born To Run': "The release date is just one day," cautioned Bruce. "The record is forever."

Landau, by now a full-time member of the inner circle, grew frustrated with the delays, and impatient with Springsteen's own reluc-

tance to finish the record. Landau snapped when at one point Springsteen decided to scrap his third album and substitute it with songs taped from forthcoming live shows. "Look," chided Landau, "you are not supposed to like it. You think Chuck Berry sits around listening to 'Maybelline'? And when he does hear it, don't you think that he wishes a few things could be changed? C'mon, it's time to put the record out."

Provisional titles included 'American Summer', 'The Legend Of Zero & Blind Terry', 'From The Churches To The Jails', 'War & Roses', 'The Hungry & The Hunted'. But everyone knew that there could only ever be one title after they had heard the single.

On its release, 'Born To Run' cemented itself as one of the key albums of the decade. There were weak links – the jerky 'Tenth Avenue Freeze-Out', the uncharacteristically *cinéma vérité* 'Meeting Across The River' and the shallow 'She's The One'. But at its best, 'Born To Run' conveyed an epic grandeur and Big Screen rock'n'roll which hadn't been heard since Phil Spector's teen symphonies of the early Sixties. The title track offered exhilaration and opportunity. The album spoke of gritting your teeth to get through the day, but revelling in the freedom offered by the highway and street corner. Springsteen took everyday characters, incidents and locations, and transformed them into myth.

Columbia Records are believed to have laid out between $100,000 and $150,000 on promoting 'Born To Run', an unheard-of amount to spend on a relative unknown. But the sum would be more than matched by the hysterical press coverage which surrounded Springsteen around the time of the album's release.

The extent of Springsteen's celebrity became apparent late in 1975, when he became the first non-political figure to feature simultaneously on the covers of both *Time* and *Newsweek* magazines. Though in the minds of some critics, such blanket exposure only confirmed that Bruce Springsteen was nothing more than a media fabrication .

Manager Mike Appel was confident that his boy would remain on the straight and narrow: "If I had a weak artist, I'd be a nervous wreck because of all the attention. But I've got Bruce Springsteen. That's why I know the *Time* and *Newsweek* covers will be to our

advantage… Hollywood couldn't have manufactured a better story. If there was any hyping, it was the press hyping itself. All I did was co-ordinate it. They came to us."

It had been a long, hard drive. 'Born To Run' finally transformed Springsteen from East Coast cult to world star, but there was a heavy price to pay. Aggrieved by the way Landau had muscled in, Mike Appel decided to take legal action which effectively kept Springsteen from releasing a follow-up for three long years.

Rock had never sounded more exultant and celebratory and joyous than it did when Bruce Springsteen drove off down 'Thunder Road' and exulted: "It's a town full of losers, and we're pulling out of here to win." The album had taken its toll, but he had survived.

THUNDER ROAD

At one point Springsteen envisaged 'Born To Run' as a – *gulp* – 'concept album'. It was scheduled to have a 'day in the life' theme, beginning with an alarm clock and an acoustic version of 'Thunder Road', ending up late in the day with a full band version of the same song. Mercifully, wisdom prevailed, and 'Born

To Run' kicks off with a full-throated rocker. Car imagery rampant, Springsteen tore into 'Thunder Road' with all the tenacity of a terrier with a leg of lamb. Performed at virtually every E.Street Band show since its release, the version which found its way onto 'Live 1975 - 85' was a stark, stripped down version, with Bruce accompanied only by Roy Bittan's mournful piano. The Roy Orbison homage in the first verse was a further testament to the influence on Bruce's work of those who had gone before. 'Thunder Road' was also the title of a 1958 film about bootlegging starring Robert Mitchum.

TENTH AVENUE FREEZE-OUT

One of those Big Apple melodramas that Springsteen can churn out by the yard. Strong-fisted brass from Clemons (whose joining the E.Street Band features in the third verse) plus top-rated session men the Brecker brothers and saxophonist David Sanborn. The song reappeared regularly during the 1988 tour to promote 'Tunnel Of Love'.

NIGHT

Back on the road again, 'Night' has similarities with 'Factory' on Springsteen's fourth album. Outside the factory gates, the only freedom lies in the highway, and the life lived outside working hours, managing to survive until the weekend. Indeed, many of the terms of reference here will figure again prominently in 'Darkness On The Edge Of Town'.

BACKSTREETS

'Backstreets' is one of those big songs which fuel 'Born To Run'. This was Springsteen writ large, the sort of rock'n'roll record that hadn't been heard on the airwaves since they had bounced off Phil Spector's Wall Of Sound a decade before. The piano and organ of Roy Bittan (rescued from the pit orchestra of *Jesus Christ Superstar*) usher in Clemons' sultry saxophone and Springsteen's raw-throated vocal. All the Bruce hallmarks are here: the intense infatuation, the precision of location, the street gangs, the loyalty, the cars... A storming version from Bruce's 1978 Roxy residency appears on 'Live 1975 - 85'.

BORN TO RUN

Springsteen's sole entry in The Oxford Dictionary Of Modern Quotations. In his own words: "My shot at the title. A 24-year-old kid aiming at 'the greatest rock'n'roll record ever'".

'Born To Run' is probably still the one song most associated with Bruce Springsteen, although incredibly in 1975, it only ever reached No. 23 on the American charts. Allan Clarke of The Hollies made history and the first cover of a song by Bruce Springsteen, when

he recorded the song in 1974, a full year before Springsteen's own version. Frankie Goes To Hollywood recorded the song for their début album. Bruce returned to the song during his 1988 tour, performing it solo, slower and stripped down, a reflection 13 years on, of the couple, now married. It was this version which finally made its UK chart début in 1987.

Few rock'n'roll songs can match the exhilaration and the sheer, resurgent magnificence of 'Born To Run'. It is the ultimate song of escape, of liberation from life's weary tedium, with a simple, four-note octave riff that takes the towering chorus towards a delirious, unforgettable high. And nowhere in rock is there a count-in as uplifting as Springsteen's manic charge into the final verse after Clarence's solo. In 1994, in a poll conducted by The Times and Radio One, 'Born To Run' was voted the greatest song of all time, just beating 'Like A Rolling Stone'. In an interview with Radio One's Trevor Dann, Springsteen remembered writing it in Long Branch in 1974. He also admitted that there was no such thing as a "drone". Looking back on the song as it appeared on the 'Live 1975-85' box, Springsteen told Dave Marsh: "The most important thing is the question thrown back at 'Born To Run' – 'I wanna know if love is real'. And the answer is yes".

SHE'S THE ONE

Jerky and staccato, an early version of the song included lyrics which later wound up in 'Backstreets', as well as filching from Springsteen's own 'Hey Santa Anna'. Released as the B-side of the 'Tenth Avenue Freeze-Out' single, 'She's The One' is a love song of fierce, possessive intensity, even if it's not up in the all-time-best-ever Bruce pantheon. "I wrote 'She's The One' because I wanted to hear Clarence play the sax in that solo. I sort of went back and wrote the words to it just cause I wanted to hear that beat and hear Clarence play that".

MEETING ACROSS THE RIVER

Bruce goes out and plays with the gangsters. A hand-held, black and white, *film noir* account of life on the wrong side of the tracks. Lacking the urgency of Lou Reed's 'Waiting For The Man', 'Meeting Across The River' is nonetheless a more considered depiction of a drug deal. Instrumentally sparse and stripped-down, 'Meeting Across The River' is another uncharacteristic Springsteen song. At least he had the courage to try something different, but file next to 'Wild Billy's Circus Story'.

JUNGLELAND

The inherent strength of the song lies in Bittan's piano and Clemons' saxophone, the foundation of another great Springsteen epic. Following on from the characters introduced on 'Incident On 57th Street', 'Jungleland' is familiar Springsteen territory – sleek machines sprint across the New Jersey state line, midnight gangs assemble, guitars are flashed like switch-blade knives. But there is a loneliness at the heart of this togetherness. For all the florid romanticism, there is a weary resignation in Springsteen's voice as he revisits the divided turf of Romeo & Juliet. This was Springsteen's opera out on the Turnpike. Listen carefully, and in 'Jungleland' you can hear the wide screen, Wagnerian high rock opera concept of 'Bat Out Of Hell'.

Bruce
Springsteen

Darkness
on the Edge
of Town

DARKNESS ON THE EDGE OF TOWN

(COLUMBIA CDCBS 86061; RELEASED: JUNE 1978)

Even with the knockout blow of 'Born To Run' and the double whammy of *Time* and *Newsweek*, the realisation was dawning that after a decade of striving for it, Bruce Springsteen was in danger of losing whatever 'it' was, and all because of a dumb contract.

It was down to the deal that Springsteen had signed in a parking lot in 1972. Back then he had nothing to lose, now it was to keep him out of the recording studio for three long years. Manager Mike Appel had grown increasingly estranged from Springsteen, who was relying more and more on Jon Landau for advice. Springsteen was concerned that Appel was underpaying him on recording royalties and wanted Landau on board in time for his fourth album. After making a payment in 1976, Appel stands firm, reluctant to lose his grip on his protégé.

Meanwhile, with his future uncertain and the prospect of being unable to release anything he does record, Springsteen puts the fourth album on hold. By his standards, 1977 is pretty much of a lost year, with only a handful of shows, including unannounced guest spots with rockabilly singer Robert Gordon, Patti Smith and Southside Johnny & The Asbury Jukes.

Despite only having three studio albums to draw on, Springsteen had dozens of unrecorded or unreleased songs of his own, as well as his enormous mental jukebox to provide new material for concerts. Live between 1975 - 78, Bruce Springsteen seemed like a living, breathing history of rock'n'roll. He majored on mid-Sixties British Invasion material, as well as the songs which had so influenced The Beatles, the Stones and The Who.

For many years, Springsteen used to include Manfred Mann's 'Pretty Flamingo', The

Searchers 'When You Walk In The Room', 'Twist & Shout', Them's 'Gloria', Bobby Fuller's 'I Fought The Law', The Animals 'It's My Life' and most nights would end up with Mitch Ryder & The Detroit Wheels' 'Devil With The Blue Dress' and 'Jenny Take A Ride' ('The Detroit Medley', which became the first official live Bruce Springsteen material available, when it was released as part of the No Nukes triple LP package in 1979).

The most regular cover in any Springsteen show was Gary 'US' Bonds' 'Quarter To Three', a staple of virtually every Bruce show from 1974 until 1981. Bonds was down to singing at McDonald's openings, when Springsteen's covers renewed interest in his career – Springsteen went on to write for and co-produce two of Bonds' comeback albums during the early 1980s.

It was during these years away from the studio that Springsteen honed and perfected his live show, and with the E.Street Band able to call up any one of a couple of hundred songs at the drop of a plectrum, Springsteen cemented his reputation as rock's premier live performer during exhausting tours of his homeland.

But however energising the live shows were, Springsteen badly needed to get back in the studio to consolidate his success with a new album, but he still had all the business problems with Appel to sort out. By his own admission, Springsteen was no business-man: "What did I know? I didn't know what publishing was!... I knew no one who had ever made a record before. I knew no one who had ever had any contact whatsoever with the music business."

It all seemed a long way from a career which began because, as Bruce admitted: "We wanted to play because we wanted to meet girls, make a ton of dough and change the world a little bit."

In 1981, Springsteen was to reflect on the case: "He (Appel) worked hard for a long time, we all worked hard, and he sacrificed and, okay, he deserved something for it. But what I wanted was the thing itself: my songs. It got so where, if I wrote a book, I couldn't even quote my lyrics – I couldn't quote 'Born To Run'. That whole period of my life just seemed to be slipping out of my hands. That's why I started playing music in the first place – to control my life. No way was I going to let that get away."

An out of court settlement was reached with Mike Appel in May 1977. Four days later, Bruce Springsteen and Jon Landau entered Atlantic recording studios in New York, where they begin to record an album to be called 'American Madness', which went on to become 'Darkness On The Edge Of Town'.

On its release in 1978, 'Darkness On The Edge Of Town' revealed a new, darker, more introspective Springsteen. Of the album, Springsteen commented: "They're 28 to 30 years old, like my age, they're not kids any more... On 'Born To Run' there was the hope of a free ride. On 'Darkness' there ain't no free ride. You wanna ride, you gotta pay!"

The cars were still there, but not the romantic routemasters of 'Born To Run'. 'Darkness' spoke of love, faith, betrayal, trust and belief, sin and redemption.

Jon Landau felt that 'Darkness On The Edge Of Town' was Springsteen's reaction to the overwhelming success of 'Born To Run'. He told Robert Hilburn: "Bruce had no interest in whether there was anything he could call a single. He was totally committed to making a record that was true to his own feelings. When you consider he had, but didn't use, songs like

'Fire' and 'Because The Night', you've got to assume he didn't really want 'Darkness' to be that big a record. Bruce was very suspicious about success. If success was what it was like with 'Born To Run', Bruce didn't want that. He didn't want one song that could be taken out of context and interfere with what he wanted the album to represent."

On its release, the sales of 'Darkness On The Edge Of Town' came nowhere near to matching those of 'Born To Run'. To his credit, Springsteen stayed true to his vision of what he wanted.

Ten years on, Springsteen looked back on the album when he spoke to Mikal Gilmore in *Rolling Stone*: "I know that before 'Darkness', I was writing songs where people were trying to escape all the time and were also searching. But once... you break those ties to the community that you came up in, what are you going to do then?... You can get isolated if you've got a lot of dough or if you don't have much dough, whether you're Elvis Presley or whether you're sitting in front of the TV with a six-pack of beer."

Kicking off with 'Badlands', which spoke of "trouble in the heartland", Springsteen took a dark and penetrating journey across America. The songs here still sounded epic and widescreen, but spoke of day to day values in the face of crisis.

The album's two best songs – the title track and 'Racing In The Street' – were pensive and sombre reflections. The outgoing rock'n'roller was still evident on 'The Promised Land' and 'Prove It All Night', but balanced by a more mature, reflective Springsteen on 'Something In The Night' and 'Factory'.

Strong and driving as the album sounds, in hindsight Springsteen himself was disappointed with the finished result ("I over-sang. We under-played"). He occasionally, unrealistically, spoke of going in to re-record the whole album. "For me, the whole thing in 'Darkness...' is just people stretching for the light in the darkness, just people trying to hold on to the things they believe in the face of the battering from the outside."

Charles R. Cross detailed the 'Darkness On The Edge Of Town' sessions in his book *Backstreets* (Sidgwick & Jackson, 1989) and identifies at least 26 songs scheduled for the album which never made it.

Among those strong contenders were 'Fire' and 'Because The Night', which went on to become staples of Springsteen's live set; 'Talk To Me' and 'Hearts Of Stone', both of which appeared on the 1978 Southside Johnny 'Hearts Of Stone" album and 'Rendezvous' which Gary 'US' Bonds covered on his 1981 'Dedication' album. Left off at the last minute were 'Don't Look Back', 'Frankie' and 'The Promise'.

Bleak as it undeniably was, after three years away 'Darkness On The Edge Of Town' confirmed Bruce Springsteen as the premier American rock star of the Seventies.

BADLANDS

Named after Terence Malick's cult 1973 film, starring Martin Sheen as a James Dean-fixated outlaw, this storming rocker was the second single released off the album. Of the song, which later appeared on 1995's 'Greatest Hits', Springsteen wrote: "This was the record, 'Darkness On The Edge Of Town', where I figured out what I wanted to write about, the people that mattered to me, and who I wanted to be. I saw friends and family struggling to lead decent, productive

lives and I felt an everyday kind of heroism in this. Still do." Significantly, the version of 'Badlands' on the 'Live 1975 – 85' album was recorded in Arizona, the day after Ronald Reagan was elected President. Springsteen introduced the song with these words: "I don't know what you guys think about what happened last night, but I think it's pretty frightening. You guys are young, there's gonna be a lot of people depending on you coming up, so this is for you."

ADAM RAISED A CAIN

Inspired by James Dean's character in his first film, *East Of Eden* in 1955. The strong, Catholic imagery told of the conflicts between a father and a son, a subject Springsteen was well versed in ("You inherit the sins, you inherit the flames"). Springsteen allowed the song to be used on the soundtrack of John Sayles' film *Baby, It's You* – Sayles later went on to direct the videos of 'Born In The USA' and 'I'm On Fire'.

SOMETHING IN THE NIGHT

A song which Springsteen had performed live at shows during late 1976, but with different lyrics. The version on the album is bleak and unremitting – seven out of the 10 songs on 'Darkness On The Edge Of Town' deal or dwell in darkness.

CANDY'S ROOM

Began life as 'Candy's Boy', then slowly turned into this driving, relentless account of a hooker and her special client. As rock'n'roll songs about prostitutes go, it's not as good as 'Honky Tonk Women', but better than 'Roxanne'. Included on 'Live 1975 - 85'.

RACING IN THE STREET

The title owes a debt to Martha & The Vandellas' 'Dancing In The Street', it is one of Springsteen's best-ever songs. All that taut compression is there, the muggy summer night, the street as the only source of escape. Springsteen has rarely sung better, or had more sympathetic accompaniment from The E.Street Band than here. Sure, there are more

automotive references than in *Autocar* magazine, but this time there is a purpose. The racing in the street is the way out. When you have nothing and nowhere to go, it's the only place you've got left. Included on 'Live 1975 - 85', and also recorded by Queen's Roger Taylor and Emmylou Harris.

THE PROMISED LAND

The third single taken off the album. The title was part homage to Chuck Berry, whose 1965 version was a minor British hit, and was memorably covered by Dave Edmunds, Elvis Presley and Johnnie Allan. Springsteen's 'Promised Land' however is a bleaker and more demanding territory than Berry's. The driving can put the miles between you and the drabness of garage life, but it is the belief which sustains you, the faith which is the petrol. Included on 'Live 1975 - 85'.

FACTORY

One of the best-ever songs about work and the work experience. On 'Factory' Bruce comes to appreciate some of the sacrifices and loss of dignity Douglas Springsteen under-went to bring up his family. Again, there is that coiled appreciation at the song's conclusion, as the men return from work all set to do some damage after their soul-destroying day. Recorded a capella by The Arizona Smoke Review and The Flying Pickets.

STREETS OF FIRE

Walter Hill named his overblown 1984 rock-'n'roll fantasy after this Springsteen song, in the hope that Bruce would donate it for use on the soundtrack. But Bruce didn't crack, and Ry Cooder got the gig. On record, Springsteen sounds ground down, bent and broken, ending with an animal howl, somehow defiant, but made incoherent and tragically diminished.

PROVE IT ALL NIGHT

The first single from the album, 'Prove It All Night' opens with one of Springsteen's most pounding riffs, heard to particularly good effect at live shows during 1978, when Springsteen let rip with some blistering guitar. Inexplicably, not included on 'Live 1975 - 85'. The song is bookended by Roy Bittan's piano and Clarence Clemons' sax solo.

DARKNESS ON THE EDGE OF TOWN

Majestic and inspiring conclusion. 'Darkness On The Edge Of Town' has proved to be one of Springsteen's most durable songs. He brought it back into his live repertoire during the desultory 1992 tour and on into 1993, per-formed with The E.Street Band, Max Weinberg's drumming was always a delight. Included on 'Live 1975 - 85' and 1992's 'Plugged' album. In performance, this one song exemplifies the very essence of what Bruce Springsteen is about. A song about diminishing dignity, and the courage to over-come the inevitable loss of dreams as age pushes you down to the wire. On record, 'Darkness...' boasts one of the great Springsteen vocals. The gruff cry of defiance, of intention stated, comes as a noble conclu-sion to an album which was a long way removed from the sweeping buoyancy of 'Born To Run', only three years before.

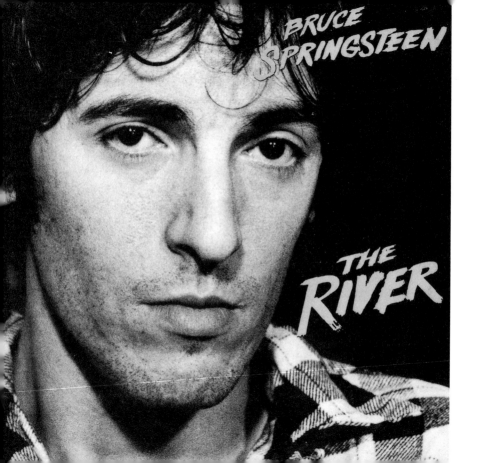

THE RIVER

(COLUMBIA, CDCBS 88510; RELEASED: OCTOBER 1980)

While the sales of 'Darkness On The Edge Of Town' didn't approach those of 'Born To Run', Springsteen was still enshrined in the hearts and minds of his American audience as The Boss. But he needed wider commercial success to match the critical hosannas which were regularly being flung his way. Springsteen had still to enjoy a Top 20 single in either the UK or the USA.

Springsteen finished touring to promote 'Darkness On The Edge Of Town' in January 1979, and returned to the studios during April of that year. The sessions which became 'The River' were, even by Springsteen's demanding standards, arduous. He had stockpiled dozens of songs, which made the sifting process more than usually difficult.

According to Charles R. Cross, in his exhaustive piece on 'The River' sessions in the Springsteen fanzine *For True Rockers Only* (issues 5 and 6), the first song recorded for the album was 'Roulette', a song inspired by the nuclear 'incident' at Three Mile Island, which never made it onto the finished album,

but appeared on the B-side of the 'One Step Up' single in 1988. 'Be True' was also scheduled for inclusion on 'The River', and that ended up as a bonus track on the 1988 'Tougher Than The Rest' single (Springsteen later admitted: "Both those songs should have been on 'The River', and I'm sure they would have been better than a couple other things that we threw on there!")

For Springsteen fans, 1979 was another 'lost' year, as he spent most of it in the studio recording. Gradually, the wealth of material was sifted down into a 10 track album 'The Ties That Bind', which in the end was never released. In its place, the following year

Springsteen released 'The River', a double album which included seven of the songs from the aborted 'Ties That Bind' project. However 'The Price You Pay' had slightly different lyrics, while the original rockabilly 'You Can Look (But You Better Not Touch)' and the earlier stately, almost minuet version of 'Stolen Car' were actually better than the versions which finally made it onto 'The River'. Two other songs from that album have yet to surface officially – 'Cindy' and 'Loose End'.

Springsteen's highest profile gig of 1979 was in September at Madison Square Garden for the MUSE (Musicians United for Safe Energy) shows. It was there that Springsteen blew the old guard (Crosby, Stills & Nash, Carly Simon and James Taylor) away, and pre-mièred a new song, 'The River'.

The majority of fans at Madison Square Garden those two nights in September, were there primarily to see Springsteen perform. By this time he had been away from the concert stage for the best part of two years, and to welcome him back, the crowd chanted a welcoming 'Brooooce'. One of the highlights of the *No Nukes* movie is Springsteen's old headliner, Bonnie Raitt, sitting in the Madison Square Garden bunker as the crowd goes crazy above, commenting "Too bad his name isn't Melvin".

Re-energised by the Madison Square Garden shows for MUSE, Springsteen had growing reservations about the finished album and put it on hold. With plans to have 'The Ties That Bind' in the shops by Christmas shelved, Springsteen went back to the studio, and spent the summer of 1980 assembling the material for a double album which would become his most successful package to date.

At the dawn of the Eighties, rock'n'roll was finally ready for Bruce Springsteen. The Rolling Stones had released another unconvincing album, David Bowie was emerging from the folly of 'Lodger' and Bob Dylan was 'born again'. It left the door open for Bruce Springsteen, who had already survived a tongue-lashing from all the young punks like The Clash and Elvis Costello.

His live shows had now grown from 90-minute sets to three and four-hour marathons, which forged a new bond between band and audience. Springsteen worked hard to create a unique sense of community at those shows, here was an Everyman with the ability to communicate on a world stage.

'The River' gave Springsteen his first real hit single: 'Hungry Heart' (originally written for The Ramones!) reached No. 5 in the States, where even 'Born To Run' had barely dented the Top 30.

Ever the perfectionist, Springsteen was driven to find the right mix of songs, properly sequenced, for his next album. Around 90 songs were written and short-listed for the album. Columbia were keen for a new record, but even they blanched as the recording costs sailed past the $500,000 mark.

The eventual double album was a real Springsteen pick'n'mix, containing some of his best work, right next to his worst. Few rock stars have sung so convincingly of breaking 'the ties that bind' as Springsteen on 'Independence Day', or more astutely about the corrosive unweaving of the American Dream than on 'The River'.

In hindsight, many of the double album's rockers have worn less well down the years, although The Searchers-sounding 'Ties That Bind', the driving 'Cadillac Ranch' and 'Sherry Darling' still sound mighty fine.

'The River' does its best to reconcile the optimism of Springsteen's third album with the weary resignation of 'Darkness On The Edge Of Town', particularly on world-weary songs such as the underrated 'The Price You Pay', the brooding 'Point Blank' and unbearably poignant 'Wreck On The Highway'.

"Rock and roll has always been this joy," reflected Springsteen around the time of the album's release, "… this certain happiness that is in its way the most beautiful thing in life. But rock is also about hardness and coldness and being alone. With 'Darkness', it was hard for me to make those things co-exist. How could a happy song like 'Sherry Darling' co-exist with 'Darkness On The Edge Of Town'? I wasn't ready for some reason within myself to feel those things. It was too confusing, too para-doxical. But I finally got to the place where I realised that life had paradoxes, a lot of them, and you've got to live with them."

This was the album which Springsteen was promoting when he finally made it back to the UK in May 1981. No one who saw Springsteen at Newcastle, Manchester, Edinburgh, Stafford, Brighton, London or Birmingham during the May and June of 1981, will ever forget the exultation of hear-ing those songs from 'The River' played live.

By then, the hype barely lived up to the actuality, and as Springsteen quit Wembley Arena after the first London show, he really had retained the crown.

It was Springsteen's naked enthusiasm which was so captivating. By the early Eighties, rock'n'roll had become as remote as it did during the progressive boom of the early Seventies, except that now it was groups like New Order playing ice-cold sets of exactly 40 minutes, or cling-film packaged pop acts going through the motions.

Bruce Springsteen came to Europe in 1981 as a rock'n'roll salvationist, and he left with a couple of hundred thousand converts. It wasn't only 'The River' material which sounded so magnificent, there was the illicit pleasure of hearing 'Fire' and 'Because The Night' played live; the thrill of hearing all the best of 'Born To Run' and 'Darkness On The Edge Of Town'; of seeing him do 'Rosalita' right in front of your face; listening to the shaggy-dog stories which prefaced the moodier songs… just being there.

There were also the covers, cherry-picked from a quarter century of rock'n'roll history – Creedence Clearwater Revival's 'Who'll Stop The Rain', The Beatles' (among others) 'Twist & Shout', Sonny Curtis' 'I Fought The Law' as energised by The Bobby Fuller Four and revitalised by The Clash. There was Elvis' 'Follow That Dream' and 'Can't Help Falling In Love', Woody Guthrie's 'This Land Is Your Land', Jimmy Cliff's 'Trapped', the Waylon Jennings/Buddy Holly 'Jole Blon' via Gary Bonds, whose 'Quarter To Three' is still a Springsteen show-stopper.

Listening to early recordings of Elvis Presley, you can hear the promise that lies in that voice, the potential which was realised in the cramped confines of Sun Studios. In concert on that tour, and in the very best of the songs on 'The River', Bruce Springsteen echoes that promise.

THE TIES THAT BIND

This pulsing rocker was strongly influenced by Jackie De Shannon's 'When You Walk In The Room' and also acknowledges Springsteen's debt to the 12-string, jingle-jangle guitars of The Searchers, the band who had such a lasting influence on The Byrds (and The Smiths and REM and…). It's a song about the sense

of community which Springsteen feels deeply and was keen to impart. Just time for a tip of the hat to Creedence's 'Who'll Stop The Rain' at the beginning of the third verse, then it's foot down on the floor all the way to the finish.

the back seat cramping his style, then it's hey, hey, hey and it's down to the beach for frolics and ice cream. Punched along by Clemons' saxophone, 'Sherry Darling' was a firm live favourite on the 1980/81 tour.

SHERRY DARLING

Originally intended for 'Darkness On The Edge Of Town', 'Sherry Darling' is frat-rock *par excellence*. Bruce beefs about mother-in-law in

JACKSON CAGE

Beginning with a fusillade of Max Weinberg drums, 'Jackson Cage' is just the sort of song Springsteen was striving for on 'The River'

("It was the first record where people were married on it"). But marriage isn't all plain sailing, and here it's a Pinteresque glimpse behind the drawn blinds of a row of houses. This isn't a relationship made in Heaven, it's a battle fought out on the killing floor.

TWO HEARTS

Fast and frenetic, 'Two Hearts' realises that alone ain't half as much fun as together. Over 30, Springsteen finally admits, on record, to "living in a world of childish dreams". Again, Mighty Max's drums draw the listener into the song. 'Two Hearts' was performed with more than usual verve during Springsteen's 1984/85 tour, when he was reunited onstage with former E.Street Band guitarist 'Miami' Steve Van Zandt.

INDEPENDENCE DAY

Another track originally intended for 'Darkness On The Edge Of Town', this song has slight echoes of Van Morrison's 1972 'Almost Independence Day' which is worth seeking out and Martina McBride's 1992 take,

'Independence Day' from her album 'The Way That I Am', is also worthy of comparison with Springsteen's masterpiece.

'Independence Day' is the great Oedipal wrecks rock'n'roll song, the flip side of Jim Morrison's 'The End'. In what is probably his best recorded vocal, Springsteen sings of his abiding love for his father and his inability to communicate that affection. The singer tells of watching the system grind the parent down, until all individuality has been squeezed out, and knowing that this must never be allowed to happen to him. As sentimental as Springsteen gets (which is going some), 'Independence Day' is as close as you get to confessional, and unerring sincerity is the power which fuels the song.

The song ebbs and flows on Danny Federici's fluting organ, the delicate acoustic guitar work and Clemons' sax break. But the over-riding image is of a teenage Bruce Springsteen, crouched in his Asbury Park bedroom, alone against the world, while downstairs, his father sits, smoking cigarette after cigarette in the darkness of his kitchen. The two men never talk, they communicate only by shouting at each other about all the bitter divisions that rule their lives and mark out the no man's land which father and son will never get to cross. When they finally do get to talk, it is Bruce Springsteen talking to Douglas from concert platforms around the world, and the world listens, and understands, everyone there has been to those lonely places, and heard those silences.

HUNGRY HEART

"My first real Top 10 smash and I guess my real entrance into the pop mainstream. I met The Ramones in Asbury Park, and Joey asked me to write a song for 'em. I went home that night and wrote this. I played it for Jon Landau and earning his money he advised me to keep it." Springsteen's first hit (US No.5; UK No.44), this version has backing vocals from former Turtles and Mothers Of Invention, Flo & Eddie. In concert, as heard on 'Live 1975-85', the whole auditorium takes the first verse. The first Springsteen song to be used on a film soundtrack – a snatch can be heard in Tom Cruise's *Risky Business.*

OUT IN THE STREET

"I wasn't going to put 'Out In The Street' on the album because it's all idealism. It's about people being together and sharing a certain feeling. I know the feeling is real, but it's hard to see sometimes. You go out in the street and there's a chance to get hit over the head or mugged. The song's not realistic in a way, but there's something very real at the heart of it". Bruce at his cockiest ("I walk the way I wanna walk") and acknowledging The Easybeats' 'Friday On My Mind', off he goes.

CRUSH ON YOU

An album filler, which comes alive in concert, but hasn't exactly worn well on record. There is, after all, only so much mileage to be extracted from a song whose chorus runs "Ooh, ooh I gotta crush on you".

YOU CAN LOOK (BUT YOU'D BETTER NOT TOUCH)

Intended for the aborted 1979 'Ties That Bind' album, in a slambang rockabilly style, this re-recorded version nonetheless remains one of

Springsteen's great high-energy rock'n'rollers, as you can hear from the version on 'Live 1975-85'. Springsteen performed the song as a solo a capella at a 1986 benefit for Neil Young's Bridge charity.

I WANNA MARRY YOU

One of Springsteen's first 'grown-up' songs, 'I Wanna Marry You' is a resigned and contemplative look at marriage and the difficulty of sustaining a relationship in a "mixed-up world". Bruce sings from the heart and recognises that in the real world, for him to say "I'll make your dreams come true would be wrong". Springsteen has always been an artist who sets great store by the sequencing of an album, which has often led to the hold up of releases until he and Landau get it just right. While it's frustrating to know that the songs are there in the can, but held up while Springsteen tinkers with the sequencing, it can work magnificently well. As with this the penultimate song on what was Side 2 of the double album: the teenage freneticism of 'Out In The Street' and 'You Can Look…' lead into the pensive and undulant 'I Wanna Marry You', and conclude with the bitter and resigned title track.

THE RIVER

It was his brother-in-law's redundancy and the effect of the recession on his nearest and dearest which made Springsteen appreciate that however liberating it was for him, rock'n'roll wasn't the answer to everything. The question "Is a dream a lie if it don't come true, or is it something worse?" is at the heart of 'The River'. "To me, the type of things that people do that make their lives heroic are a lot of times very small, little things… something between a husband and a wife… It's a grand experience, but it's not always big. There's plenty of room for those kinds of victories, and I think the records have that." Springsteen's harmonica adds extra poignancy to the tale, while Roy Bittan's piano bobs and weaves, like moonlight on water. 'The River' was the third single to be lifted off the album, there was a 12" version (which also included 'Born To Run' and 'Rosalita') the cover of which – Springsteen seated at night in a darkened petrol station – had almost made it as the cover of 'Darkness On The Edge Of Town'.

POINT BLANK

The third mention of Romeo in a Springsteen song, 'Incident On 57th Street' and 'Fire' being the others. But this Romeo is no streetwise suitor, and his Juliet just sits, blank-eyed, waiting for welfare payments. Performed live during 1978, the song was even bleaker, with a lyric based around a girlfriend's drug addiction. The title came from a hard-bitten 1967 gangster movie starring Lee Marvin. 'Point Blank' was the final song to be recorded for 'The River'. Introducing it on tour in Stockholm in 1981, Springsteen told the audience: "A song ain't no good until somebody hears it. By yourself you can't have an effect. You have to reach out. This is a song about someone who loses that power, which is the most powerful thing in the world – your ability to affect your friends' lives… and my life".

CADILLAC RANCH

'Cadillac Ranch' itself is situated in Amarillo, Texas, appropriately just off Route 66. Springsteen can be seen cavorting among the Cadillacs, all buried hood-deep in the dust, in the Born In The USA tour brochure. Another one of those 1981 in-concert favourites which featured on 'Live 1975-85', it always signalled an opportunity for Clemons to take the spotlight and let rip a mighty sax solo. Among Springsteen's most blatant car songs, one of the Cadillacs was exhumed, given a re-spray and resurfaced as 'Pink Cadillac', which was the B-side to 1984's 'Dancing In The Dark' single.

I'M A ROCKER

Fast and frenetic, 'I'm A Rocker' namechecks lotsa TV cop shows (*Columbo, Kojak, Mission Impossible*), and uh, that's it. Fun in concert, it usually appeared right at the end of a blistering 28 song evening, always an up note to end on, prior to the exhausting encores.

FADE AWAY

Baffling choice for second single to come off the album, 'Fade Away' only reached USA No. 20 and wasn't released in Europe. In 1964, The Rolling Stones had insisted that they 'Not Fade Away', but Bruce is more pleading, he copes with the end of something by praying that there can be a fresh beginning. It's a wish born out of desperation though, and the likelihood is that he will end up spent, "just another useless memory". Discarded, and all faded.

STOLEN CAR

Brooding and melancholic, 'Stolen Car' is another Bruce Springsteen car song, but this time you believe him when he says: "I don't write songs about cars. My songs are about people in those cars". In tone and atmosphere, 'Stolen Car' is similar to a vintage Robert Mitchum *film noir* – *Build My Gallows High* perhaps. Springsteen had rarely sounded more mournful as he chronicled the breakdown of a marriage. The character's only escape is racing through the streets by night, but this time around, the freedom promised by 'Racing In The Streets' in 1978 is gone, this time out, he is driving a stolen car, aimlessly, bitterly, drifting down the darkened streets, just waiting to get caught.

RAMROD

Springsteen carries on motorvating, but flicks the switch: 'Ramrod' has all the ebullience and knowing familiarity of a Chuck Berry car song, none of the pointless, sombre, confessional motoring of 'Stolen Car'. Another live favourite, 'Ramrod' again gave Bruce the opportunity to focus the spotlight on Clarence

Clemons. And while 'Ramrod' is no more than a 4-star, gas-fuelled, hot-stepping rock'n'roll fragment, nobody does it better.

THE PRICE YOU PAY

One of Springsteen's most undervalued songs, tucked away on the fourth side of 'The River', 'The Price You Pay' is a dignified and stately piece. Uncharacteristically Biblical in tone, the song shows how well Springsteen is capable of building and developing a song, packing an emotional punch at the conclusion of every verse. Listen to the way Springsteen handles the chorus at the end of the third verse, punctuates it with a harmonica solo, then limps into the bridge ("Little girl down on the strand…"). It's familiar Springsteen turf – chosen lands, promised lands, riverbanks, county lines – territory he stalks and claims as his own, particularly on a song as strong as this. 'The Price You Pay' was covered by Emmylou Harris on her 1981 album Cimmaron, which also bafflingly included a Paul Kennerley song 'Born To Run'.

DRIVE ALL NIGHT

Overblown and histrionic, 'Drive All Night' typifies the worst excesses of Springsteen on 'The River'. Mistaking repetition and poor diction for conviction and intensity, Springsteen promises to drive all night – for a pair of shoes!

WRECK ON THE HIGHWAY

Then, in a bravura sleight of hand, Springsteen brings it all back home, with the subdued and eerily majestic 'Wreck On The Highway'. Country-tinged (Roy Acuff had a hit with the same title in 1944), 'Wreck On The Highway' distills the essence of what makes Bruce Springsteen great: a looping, loping and involving melody, heartfelt vocal and acutely visual lyrics. By focusing on a specific incident, an accident observed casually from a passing car, Springsteen broadens the song in its final verse to contemplate the ultimate questions of life and death. It is a brilliantly evocative, cinematic song. A subdued and moving winding down with which to conclude a sprawling and intriguing collection.

NEBRASKA

(COLUMBIA CBS 4633602; RELEASED: SEPTEMBER 1982)

Between the rock of 'The River' and the hard place of 'Born In The USA' was 'Nebraska', an album born of personal frustration and political dissatisfaction. It is quite the starkest and most confessional album Bruce Springsteen has ever recorded. It is also, quite possibly, the best album Springsteen has ever recorded.

The music on 'Nebraska' is as stark and black and white as its cover photograph. It is quite uncharacteristic Springsteen, which is perhaps why it finds such favour with long-term fans, who find some solace in its openness and frankness. It is Bruce Springsteen the way John Hammond first envisaged him 10 years before, a minstrel, stalking the byways and backwaters of America, armed only with a songwriter's eye and an acoustic guitar.

Springsteen had swerved confidently between exultant, out and out rockers and sombre ballads on 'The River'. 'Nebraska' just stripped the carcass down to the bone, there was no flesh on the album, it is raw, exposed and intimate; dark and pensive. 'Nebraska' is the rogue card in the deck of Springsteen albums. To fully appreciate its impact, to put it into some sort of perspective, you have to go right back, back a decade, back before Perestroika and tiramisu, back before CD and DCC, back before a Democrat occupied 1600 Pennsylvania Avenue. Back to January 3, 1982...

Ronald Reagan had been a personally popular but politically disastrous President for barely a year, the day that Bruce Springsteen sat down to demo the 10 songs which would eventually become the 'Nebraska' album. Reagan's affability and genuine good humour masked his economic hawkishness and an unwillingness to recognise the social evils which were the result of his harsh economic policies.

In conjunction with Margaret Thatcher, his comrade-in-arms across the Atlantic, Reagan's Presidency marked a swing to the Right. The Reagan era meant that being born in the USA during the Eighties was a risky business. The Western world was gearing up for an unprecedented boom, which would peak with the stock market crash of 1987, and lead to the worst depression since the 1930s.

'Nebraska' was released before the second Great Depression began to bite, but the voice which comes from the album is already disillusioned and cynical. It is a voice which recognises that when the economy crumbles, it's those at the bottom of the heap who get crushed first, not those sliding down from the top.

The predominant tone of the 'Nebraska' songs is world-weary and bitter, ironic when you consider that they came from a man then at the peak of his professional career: 'The River' had been Springsteen's most successful album to date, with 'Hungry Heart' finally garnering him that first elusive Top 10 hit. It was also the album which gave him financial stability after years of getting by on critical approval.

You'd never guess that two years down the road from that success, easing off the

burgeoning Boss-mania, Springsteen would sit down alone at home and pour his heart into a Teac tape recorder, or that from those pared down and chillingly effective songs would come as compelling and poignant a comment on the Reagan Years as any in print, on record or film.

The reason that 'Nebraska' still stands out and did not disappear like the President whose policies inspired it, is that it remains Springsteen's most honest and affecting album. On these songs, there is nowhere for Bruce Springsteen to run, there's nowhere for the narrator to hide. What you hear is largely what you get: one man, one guitar, 10 songs. There is none of the hollow bombast of 'You Can Look...' or the lengthy emptiness of 'Drive All Night'. 'Nebraska' is as good as it gets, as honest and direct, as open as Bruce Springsteen can make it.

To fully appreciate 'Nebraska', you have to put it in the context of what else was out there at the time. The world had Springsteen cast in stone as a rocker, 'Nebraska' was the curve ball. Nobody had heard an acoustic guitar on national radio for 20 years. By 1982, the predominant airwave sound was the synthesiser, it was the era of silly haircuts and twiddly, robot pop.

America was on the receiving edge of a second 'British Invasion' - Freddie & The Dreamers replaced by A Flock Of Seagulls; then there were Eurythmics, Heaven 17, Yazoo and Culture Club. What America did not expect was a solo acoustic guitar strummed not just by a man, but strummed by 'The Boss'.

The desperation which drove Springsteen to 'Nebraska' was personal and judgemental. It was an album which took the pressure off him and offered the opportunity to reflect on wider issues. It was a state of the nation address, delivered from a ditch by the side of a highway.

"'Nebraska' was rock bottom," Springsteen reflected on the album five years later. "I always think of it as my most personal record. What happens when all the things you believe in when you're 25 don't work? What happens when all these things break down? Your friends fail you, or you fail your friends. When you're alone – can you live? Can you go on?"

A sense of governmental failings and of individuals crushed by an uncaring society fills the album, which is populated by a motley cast of nonconformists, misfits and failures. Springsteen's belief that the man who "turns his back on his family, well he just ain't no good"

seemed now to be flying in the face of all the evidence – the failure of personal relationships and the very ties that bind, being at the core of all the other, broader failures. But it's touching that Springsteen still believed salvation lay in the family. By the time 'Nebraska' was released, families all over America were getting their wagons in a circle, and bracing themselves for crack epidemics, AIDS and the sharp end of Reaganomics. Nothing was holding up.

Although the title track deals with the Charlie Starkweather murders of 1959 (detailed in Terence Malick's brilliant 1973 film *Badlands*), it still resonated strongly in 1982. While the whole feel of the album is of a grainy, black and white Fifties movie, the sentiments are timeless, resounding with a contemporary relevance over the parched landscapes of the early Reagan years.

Because it is effectively a 'folk' album, 'Nebraska' is always direct and accessible. Folk music is the music of the people, by the people and for the people. It lives and breathes, changes and endures down the centuries because it is easy to appreciate and digest. There is no shame in making a folk record, everybody's done it, from Bob Dylan to

Elvis Costello, from R.E.M. to Van Morrison; but swirling in the rich elixir that is 'Nebraska' are strains of other American music. Jimmie Rodgers 'The Singing Brakeman', whose plaintive yodels evoke lonesome train whistles on faraway tracks, the harsh blues of the Mississippi delta, preached by the fiery Robert Johnson and the desolate Country & Western of Hank Williams, echoes of all these percolate the record. For something so stark and simple, there is a richness and texture to 'Nebraska' which – try as he might – Springsteen has rarely been able to replicate.

'Tunnel Of Love' lay five years ahead, equally bleak and desolate, but it lacks the strength of 'Nebraska' because it is a much more personal cry from the heart – the guy's marriage was falling apart and the only way he knew how to respond was to make an album about it. The songs of 'Nebraska' deal with broader issues, the tragedy of a society breaking apart rather than the failure of one relationship. 'Nebraska' is a look at the underdogs, those who have been let down by the very society in which they placed so much faith. These are people who cannot sustain a relationship with anyone – lover, parent, brother, sister. The citizens of Springsteen's 'Nebraska' are individuals at the onset of the Eighties, who – through no fault of their own – simply can't cope.

On 'Nebraska' there is a wider horizon to strive toward, as the two-lane highway flexes out into the badlands of Wyoming, a solitary car drives on into the sunset. Inside, the radio is jammed with gospel stations, but switching the dial as the sun sinks in your rear view mirror, the sound of a plaintive, lonely voice starts singing about a girl twirling her cheerleader's baton on her father's front lawn. And as you drive ever forwards, you are drawn into that world, and the journey can begin all over again.

'Nebraska' stands as Springsteen's most open and honest album. The songs were only intended as simple demos for the E.Street Band to work from, but the longer rehearsals progressed, the more Springsteen was drawn back to his own stark solo acoustic versions. Stripped down and confessional, there was nowhere to run, nowhere to hide behind in these 10 songs. While effectively alienating the 'Hungry Heart' crowd, 'Nebraska' re-established Springsteen as the critics' favourite.

Johnny Cash covered two songs from the album, and the ghosts of veteran bluesmen and country singers stalk the black and white world of 'Nebraska'. Springsteen never sounded more desperate than here. It is an album shot full of desperation, personal and political; the characters here have been ground down by Reaganomics, and can find little salvation in their crumbling relationships.

"In a funny way," Springsteen remembered five years after the album's release, "I always considered it my most personal record, because it felt to me, in its tone, the most what my childhood felt like. Later on, a bunch of people wrote about it as a response to the Reagan era, and it obviously had that connection."

At around the time of 'Nebraska', Springsteen himself experienced some sort of crisis: "There was a particular moment when I said 'Oh, my ideas that have sustained me have sort of failed'. I had a particular time when I felt pretty empty and very isolated, and I suppose that's where some of that record came from."

"It became obvious fairly soon," recalled E.Street Band drummer Max Weinberg, "that what Bruce wanted on the record was what he already had on the demo. The band, though we played the hell out of them, tended to obscure the starkness and the vibe he was going for."

'Nebraska' was uncompromising, here was Bruce Springsteen as solo singer/songwriter, standing alone with a guitar and weaving his stories. However, this was only one side of the picture, and it proved to be just the calm before the storm.

Springsteen hadn't intended 'Nebraska' to be his first solo album. It was made at his rented home at Colt's Neck, New Jersey, on January 3, 1982, the songs having been written in the months leading up to Christmas 1981. Recording his vocals and guitar direct onto a new toy, a Teac 4-track portastudio, Springsteen filled the remaining two tracks with overdubs (some guitar, synthesiser, echo, harmony) and stuffed the finished tape into his back pocket.

Try as he might, he could never – solo or with the band – recreate the mood he had evoked at home that January day, and those bleak and desolate songs became 'Nebraska'. "It just seemed to be a mood that I was in at the time... I knew I wanted to make a certain type of record, but I certainly didn't plan to make that record."

The characters on 'Nebraska' exist in a vacuum, operating outside the law or the family, adrift on the periphery of society, outcasts on a road stretching towards a flat and desolate horizon.

"That's one of the most dangerous things, I think – isolation," Springsteen told *Rolling Stone* two years after the release of 'Nebraska'. "What happens to people when they're alienated from their friends and their community and their government and their job. Because those are the things that keep you sane… and if they slip away and you start to exist in some void where the basic constraints of society are a joke, then life becomes kind of a joke, and anything can happen."

NEBRASKA

Inspired by a 1973 Martin Sheen film *Badlands*, which Springsteen saw on TV one night at the end of the 'The River' tour. The film detailed the real-life killing spree of Charlie Starkweather and his girlfriend Caril Fugate during 1958. Unusually for Springsteen, he sat down and exhaustively researched the song – reading as much as he could about the events and calling up the author of a book on the Starkweather murders. Indeed, much of the 'Nebraska' album came about following Springsteen's reading of a *History Of The United States*, which had given him a fresh perspective into the economic and social forces which had shaped his country.

The song's arresting opening lines ("I saw her standin' on her front lawn, just twirlin' her baton…") come directly from Malick's film, where Sheen's first glimpse of Sissy Spacek is on her father's lawn practising her cheerleader's baton twirls. The inherent chill of the album's title song comes from Springsteen's flat vocal, whether telling of the murder of 10 innocent people or the narrator's own death, the vocal remains as cool and unemotional as a traffic report. In tone and content, 'Nebraska' is reminiscent of the documentary-style film *Henry, Portrait Of A Serial Killer*. 'Nebraska' is as flat and barren as the badlands of Eastern Wyoming, the killing fields where Charlie Starkweather and his girl wrought havoc during 1958.

ATLANTIC CITY

'Atlantic City' deals with the sort of low-rent gangsters who had featured in Louis Malle's 1981 film starring Burt Lancaster and Susan Sarandon. It was the first Springsteen song to be promoted by a video: a grainy black & white promo, featuring shots of Atlantic City's boardwalk, with no sign of Bruce at all. The song scuffs around with small-time gangsters and hustlers, its protagonist is sucked into their world, tired of always being a loser, and by the last verse there is little doubt what sort of "favour" he has in mind. There is none of the glamorised criminality of 'Meeting Across The River' here; like so much of the album, 'Atlantic City' is hand-held black and white. 'Atlantic City' was the first (European only) single released from the album, but made no impression on the UK charts.

MANSION ON THE HILL

Hank Williams' had a hit called 'Mansion On The Hill' in 1948, one of his most affecting tunes and Springsteen was on a Hank Williams jag while writing 'The River' and leading up to 'Nebraska'. Bruce's song is based on a real location he and his father used to visit during his adolescence, and that childhood sense of wonder is maintained during the song. It's also a song of envy, the coiled-up blue-collar inhabitants of Springsteen's 1978 song 'Factory' spill out of the gates, and drive past the steel gates which keep them out of the opulent mansion. 'Mansion On The Hill' is one of the album's most cinematic songs – the fourth verse evoking the sort of parties F. Scott Fitzgerald described in *The Great Gatsby*, while in interview, Springsteen admitted that the 1962 film *To Kill A Mockingbird* played a part in the shaping of the song.

JOHNNY 99

Despite its almost jaunty tune and Springsteen's ebullient performance, 'Johnny 99' is as bleak as any song on 'Nebraska'. Unemployment, penury, robbery, attempted murder and probable public execution are all that's on offer. Unlike the mindless psychopath on the album's title song, 'Johnny 99' provides motivation: with the auto plant closed down, debt looming, the bank calling in his mortgage… Ralph accepts his prison sentence, but anticipates worse. He recognises that things aren't going to get any better. The song provided Johnny Cash with the title of his 1983 album, an album which also included a cover of 'Highway Patrolman'. Cash was old enough to remember the effects of the Great Depression first time around and his versions of the songs have an added gravitas to them.

HIGHWAY PATROLMAN

'Highway Patrolman' is the most affecting song on the album. This is the story of Cain and Abel relocated to Michigan, close up by the wintry Canadian border. "I'm not my brother's keeper," mumbled James Dean in *East Of Eden*, Hollywood's 1955 retelling of Cain & Abel. But according to Springsteen, he is, we all are. Blood is undeniably thicker than water, whatever you go through, the person you really are is inevitably shaped by where, and who, you come from – "Man turns his back on his family, well he just ain't no good."

Of all the songs on 'Nebraska', 'Highway Patrolman' is the most considered, the most finished. Springsteen's voice aches with emotion as he details the wrongdoings of his feckless brother, and you sympathise, because you know things are just never going to change. 'Highway Patrolman' has Springsteen involved, mournful and heartfelt, quite the opposite of the detached narrator on 'Nebraska'. Even on the finished track, you can hear Springsteen's chair creaking, which adds to the homely feel of the album. In a rare reversal, this song inspired Sean Penn's 1991 film *The Indian Runner*.

STATE TROOPER

The New Jersey Turnpike was where Simon & Garfunkel counted the cars in 'America' and where Jack Kerouac set off on the road. Springsteen's staccato song captures the headache-inducing tension of late-night car rides, with blinding headlights and shock-jocks jamming the airwaves. The tension and atmosphere are highlighted by Springsteen's solo, jagged guitar. 'State Trooper' was covered by

Steve Earle on his 1989 single 'Back To The Wall' and was also recorded by The Cowboy Junkies on their 1986 début album 'Whites Off Earth Now!'

USED CARS

The most obviously autobiographical song on the record. In concert, Springsteen had a boot full of memories with which to regale his audience: of driving endlessly around New Jersey over weekends, with his father at the wheel, his sister in the front seat and his mother uncomplaining in the back. 'Used Cars' was also the title of a 1980 Robert Zemeckis film.

OPEN ALL NIGHT

More songs about cars and… carburettors. Another claustrophobic driving song, with the radio waves full of relentless gospel stations. The final lines find Springsteen lapsing into incoherent, blissful praise of rock'n'roll. Released as 'Nebraska's' second single, but even with the otherwise unavailable 'Big Payback' – recorded at the 'Nebraska' sessions – as a B-side, it still failed to chart.

MY FATHER'S HOUSE

Springsteen recalled that Charles Laughton's 1955 dark masterpiece *Night Of The Hunter* was the inspiration for this sombre song, which is a companion piece to the earlier 'Mansion On The Hill'. The subdued, Biblical feel of the song echoes the title's origins in The Gospel According To St John: "In my Father's house are many mansions". It is also among the album's most overtly personal songs.

Springsteen's rollercoaster relationship with his father has been a constant theme of his work: "A lot of those songs are connected," he admitted to Robert Hilburn, "Take 'Adam Raised A Cain', 'Independence Day', 'My Father's House' – if you play those three songs together, you'll see somebody grow up." And try as he might to squash his Catholic upbringing, its legacy can be heard when in the last line of the song, Springsteen sings of a place "where our sins lie unatoned". The song was covered by Emmylou Harris on her '13' album in 1987.

REASON TO BELIEVE

The tragic Tim Hardin also wrote a song called 'Reason To Believe' which Rod Stewart covered on the multi-platinum 'Every Picture Tells A Story', though it brought no comfort to Hardin who had sold all his song copyrights to buy drugs. He died a poor, bloated heroin addict in 1980. Springsteen's 'Reason To Believe' was an ambiguous song about faith: was he mocking people's desire to believe, or envying it? To Dave Marsh, Springsteen confessed that "'Reason To Believe'… that was the bottom. I would hope not to be in that particular place ever again. It was a thing where all my ideas might have been working musically, but they were failing me personally."

There is an ambiguity in the song. Part of it is steeped in the Victorian ideal of Christian faith, which the rich, ruling classes distil into you: you may have a shitty time on earth, but it will all be fine when you get to Heaven. Springsteen seems to marvel that despite a horrendous life here on earth, at the end of a day which has seen death, betrayal and more death, people are still capable of finding "some reason to believe". But then the final irony, if there wasn't that faith, that belief, if that "reason to believe" was taken away from them, wouldn't their lives be even emptier?

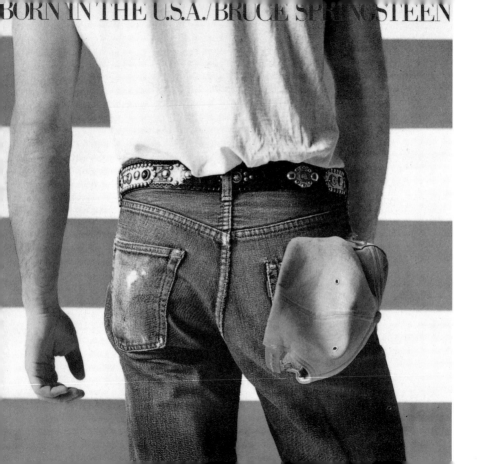

BORN IN THE U.S.A./BRUCE SPRINGSTEEN

BORN IN THE U.S.A.

(COLUMBIA, CDCOL 86304; RELEASED: JUNE 1984)

Like 'Bridge Over Troubled Water', 'Hotel California', 'Dark Side Of The Moon' and 'Rumours' before it, the album that hikes you right up the ladder isn't necessarily your best shot. 'Born In The USA' was nowhere near Bruce Springsteen's best-ever album. But it was the record which sold to people who didn't normally buy albums, which is a huge and lucrative audience to tap into. 'Born In The USA' went on to become one of the Top 10 best-selling albums of all time, with an estimated 18 million copies sold worldwide. It was the album which took Springsteen from being a man-of-the-people rock'n'roller, and propelled him into an élite cosmos – alongside Michael Jackson and Prince – as one of the biggest rock stars in the world.

"The 'Born In The USA' experience obviously had its frightening moments," Springsteen was to reflect 18 million albums later. "But I was 35, and I had a real solid sense of myself by that time. With 'Born In The USA', I had a chance to relive my 1975 experience when I was calm and completely prepared and went for it."

Springsteen had spent much of 1983 driving across America, searching for something which even the cathartic 'Nebraska' hadn't provided. Something was burning up inside Springsteen, he wasn't happy in his relationships with women (or the lack of them), he was clearly uncertain about what direction his music with The E.Street Band should be taking and he was uncertain how to commit himself to a new album from the wealth of material he had stockpiled, but was unable to sift down.

The log-jam between 'Nebraska' and 'Born In The USA' recalled Springsteen's anxious reluctance to release 'Born To Run' nearly 10 years earlier. He had shortlisted around 100 songs for the dozen tracks which would

Springsteen had included reluctantly only at the last moment, under pressure from manager Landau to include "something more commercial". Landau admits that the exchange was "by our standards, testy". Springsteen's response to his manager's request was: "Look, I've written 70 songs. You want another one – you write it!"

Following the heartfelt acoustic diversion he had taken for 'Nebraska', Springsteen knew that he had to come up with a killer rock'n'roll album to regain the audience that had drifted away between 'The River' and 'Nebraska'. Despite the bone-crunching *bonhomie* of its rock'n'roll, it is the less hysterical, more under-stated side of the album, in a direct line from 'Nebraska', which – 10 years on from its release – seems to work best. 'Downbound Train' and 'My Hometown' have much more resonance at this distance, than the bombastic 'Bobby Jean' or 'Darlington County'.

The title track had originally been recorded as part of the home-taped acoustic sessions which had resulted in 'Nebraska'. Reconvening The E.Street Band, Springsteen threw the riff to keyboardists Roy Bittan and

eventually constitute his breakthrough album. There was a clutch of good songs, and some great ones such as 'Murder In C' and 'This Hard Land', which wouldn't see the light of day until ten more years had passed.

The album's success had much to do with its lead-off single 'Dancing In The Dark', which

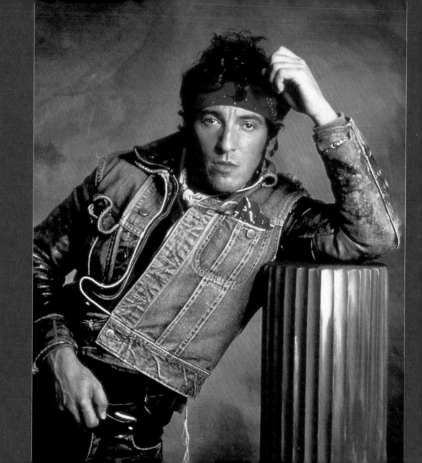

Danny Federici, who fell upon it like scavenging dogs on a bone. Drummer Max Weinberg remembers that original 'Born In The USA' session as "the greatest single experience I've ever had recording". With what was to become the title track in the can, Springsteen was off the blocks and running; a further six of the album's 12 songs ('Glory Days', 'I'm Goin' Down', 'I'm On Fire', 'Darlington County', 'Working On The Highway' and 'Downbound Train') were recorded in a three-week burst during May 1982.

Further sessions followed, but of the dozens of songs recorded between May 1982 and mid-1983, only one song – 'My Hometown' – made it on to the finished album. Other songs cut at these sessions, like 'Pink Cadillac', 'Stand On It' and 'Shut Out The Light' did however surface as B-sides.

Then, in another burst early in 1984, the rest of the album began to come together, with Springsteen and The E.Street Band cutting 'Dancing In The Dark', 'Bobby Jean' and 'No Surrender' – the latter two valedictions to guitarist Steve Van Zandt who had quit to pursue a solo career. All sorts of other songs were considered for the album: Springsteen had been toying with 'Frankie' since 1976; he had rewritten one of his favourite Elvis songs 'Follow That Dream', which was shortlisted for inclusion; a ballad called 'My Love' has still to see the light of day...

It was the album's title track which later drew the flak. Misappropriated by the political Right in America, it became a millstone for its composer, who eventually turned down an eight-figure sum for its use by Chrysler in an advertising campaign.

Brash and over the top as it sounded on the boisterous rockers like 'Working On The Highway' and 'Darlington County', the album was further proof of Springsteen's maturing. It dealt with themes previously unheard in rock-'n'roll: of just how you grow old gracefully; of what binds you to the past but shouldn't staple you to the future. Of change. Of growing up.

The subsequent tour found a newly radicalised Springsteen back in front of his loyal audience. His sympathy towards the forgotten and marginalised Vietnam veterans was heartwarming, but he took things a step further during the 1984/85 tour. Most stops in every major US city featured a comment from Bruce about local food banks, trade unions, deceptive

governments. In the UK, he was criticised in the House Of Commons for donating money to a miners' wives' strike support group.

Springsteen had even heard his name hijacked by President Reagan, which was ironic, given that the resentment which fuelled 'Nebraska' and the angrier elements of 'Born In The USA' was a direct result of Reagan's policies.

Springsteen was now welcoming the responsibility which came with his power and prestige. It was heartening to see him in action, he was broadening his horizons, not relying on a glorious back catalogue to sustain him, but forging ahead. The success of 'Born In The USA' was unexpected, although both he and Landau knew it would do better than 'Nebraska'. They had expected it to build on the commercial foothold of 'The River' and they both knew that with a contrived commercial lead-off single like 'Dancing In The Dark', they would get the airplay, but when the results started coming in, no one was prepared for the scale of its success.

At the conclusion of the 15-month world tour, Springsteen retired to take stock. Even he admitted to being "Bruced out" by it all. He was one of the very few who did not succumb to the album's charms: "I never really felt like I quite got it." He was in the minority though, and he would learn to bite the bullet about what he saw as the album's flaws. One estimate had Springsteen earning a quarter of a billion dollars from the album, tour and merchandising. No wonder *The Wall Street Journal* called him "perhaps the most influential American rock artist since Elvis Presley."

BORN IN THE USA

A third take, cut live in the studio, the song was inspired by Springsteen's experience of working with Vietnam veterans. He had avoided the draft in the mid-Sixties, but the drummer from his first band had died in combat in Vietnam. In 1987, Springsteen spoke about how "Vietnam turned this whole country into a dark street, and unless we can walk down those dark alleys and look into the eyes of those men and women, we are never gonna get home". The song was inspired by Ron Kovic's memoir *Born On The 4th Of July* (which had also been part of the inspiration for 'Racing In The Street').

'Born In The USA' is based on a powerful, six note, chiming riff that rings ominously on an open top string, echoing the melody and holding the song together like a clenched fist. It was used to open the shows on the concurrent tour, when Bruce, now boasting the physique of a weightlifter, would bring it to a terrific climax with a series of lurching false endings and and spiralling guitar solos. It had begun life in the batch of songs that Springsteen taped at home in January 1982 and which later formed the basis of 'Nebraska'. The title came from a script passed to Springsteen by director Paul Schrader who was hoping for a title song for his movie. Bruce kept the title, and Schrader got 'Light Of Day'. In 1990, Springsteen allowed 2 Live Crew to use the melody of 'Born In The USA' for their 'Banned In The USA' single. He also allowed the song to be heard over the end credits of the 1987 documentary *Dear America*, authorising its use with the words: "Take it – it's their song anyway".

COVER ME

Originally written for Donna Summer, Landau astutely recognised the song's commercial potential and Donna had to settle for Bruce's 'Protection'. Released as the second single from the album, 'Cover Me' reached No. 16 (UK) and No. 7 (USA). Arthur Baker also had fun with this one, remaking it on a 48-track console, the six-minute 'undercover mix' was stunning.

DARLINGTON COUNTY

Work had actually begun on the song as far back as 'Darkness On The Edge Of Town' in 1978. It's standard Springsteen album fare, lots of "Sha la las…", not quite as lively as 'The Ties That Bind', but close.

WORKING ON THE HIGHWAY

Another song which started out as part of the 1982 'Nebraska' work tape. Slap bass rockabilly. Fun, despite the lyrics which speak of penitentiaries and road gangs.

DOWNBOUND TRAIN

Mournful vocal, pensive and reflective song, the first on the album. The railroad has a long tradition in American music, a symbol used often in blues, folk, country and rockabilly. In 'Downbound Train', Springsteen pays homage to the 'Midnight Special' and Hank Williams' 'I Heard That Lonesome Whistle', and perhaps even 'Mystery Train', Elvis's greatest Sun recording. There is an aching, yearning sense of space, and of all the broken dreams and spent romance carried on a train, heading down the tracks, and way, way out of sight.

I'M ON FIRE

Coiled and tense, Springsteen never sounded more sinister, more spooky, more sexually roused, than here. 'I'm On Fire' brought Side 1 of the album to a subdued but memorable close. The third single from the album, a double A-side (with 'Born In The USA'), 'I'm On Fire' reached UK No.5 (US No.6).

NO SURRENDER

One of the best ever rock'n'roll songs about rock'n'roll. Springsteen included a slowed-down solo version on the 'Live 1975-85' box set. Bruce was one of the few who really had learned more from a three minute record than he ever had in school. Though the song also accepts, romantic as the idea seems, that it is unrealistic to take on the world armed with just drums and guitars.

BOBBY JEAN

This buoyant rocker was written as an "au revoir" to Bruce's best buddy, guitarist Miami Steve Van Zandt (just try substituting 'Miami Steve' in place of the title).

I'M GOIN' DOWN

Bruce cruises, gets horny again, and acts like a frustrated teenager. The song is somewhat at odds with Springsteen's increasing political awareness of the time, sounding old fashioned and incongruous. When it came to up-and-at-'em rock'n'rollers, Springsteen had a drawer full of them, he didn't need 'I'm Goin' Down'.

GLORY DAYS

"The 1st verse actually happened," wrote Bruce in 1995, "the 2nd verse mostly happened, the 3rd verse, of course, is happening now." Fourth single from 'Born In The USA' (UK No.17; US No.5). But it sounds like they had more fun recording it than we have listening to it.

DANCING IN THE DARK

"My big smash! No.2 on the charts (damn the artist formerly known as Prince). A bunch of autograph seeking Catholic schoolgirls came rushing up to me on the streets of NYC screaming they'd seen the video. Teen idol status at 35! I enjoyed it." Actually one of Springsteen's weakest-ever singles ("I need a love reaction", really!). The success of 'Dancing In The Dark' owed much to the high rotation the video received on MTV but Springsteen's first proper promo, directed by Brian de Palma, was a contrived effort with some unconvincing miming from Bruce. In it Bruce invites a girl from the audience up on stage to dance, a scenario he enacted nightly on the 'Born In The USA' tour.

The first single from the album, this gave Springsteen his biggest ever UK hit (No.4), and his first Grammy, for Best Male Vocalist. It was also the first Springsteen single to be made available in 12″ format, benefiting from Arthur Baker 'blaster', 'dub' and 'radio' mixes. Conservative Brooooce rock'n'roll fans were not amused. They were amused, though, when Big Daddy covered the song in 1985, in the Beach Party style of Frankie Avalon.

MY HOMETOWN

"The harshness of Reaganism, post-industrial America, memories of my childhood and my town." The seventh single to be lifted off the album for the American market (they also got 'I'm Goin' Down'), 'My Hometown' reached No.6. It got to No.9 in the UK, largely, literally, on the back of the other side, the seasonal

'Santa Claus Is Comin' To Town'. 'My Hometown' is a universal favourite in concert, whether in Asbury Park, London or Stockholm; it is your hometown of which Springsteen sings, and that lends added impact to an already moving and affecting song. U2 have also featured the song in concert.

'My Hometown' continues a line begun on 'Independence Day'. Strongly autobiographical, the second verse refers to the race riots which tore through Asbury Park during the turbulent summer of 1965. The third verse continues the theme of heightened awareness which Springsteen first gave voice to on 'The River'. He once said of the song: "It's something you carry with you forever, no matter where you go or what you become. There's a lot of conflicting feelings you have about the place. That's just part of it."

'My Hometown' is a reflective conclusion, winding down an album which is too hyperbolic for its own good. The frenzy of 'Bobby Jean' and 'Cover Me' find little echo in the more subdued, contemplative ballads, which balanced out 'The River'. 'Born In The USA' may be Bruce Springsteen's best-*selling* album. but it is not Bruce Springsteen's *best* album.

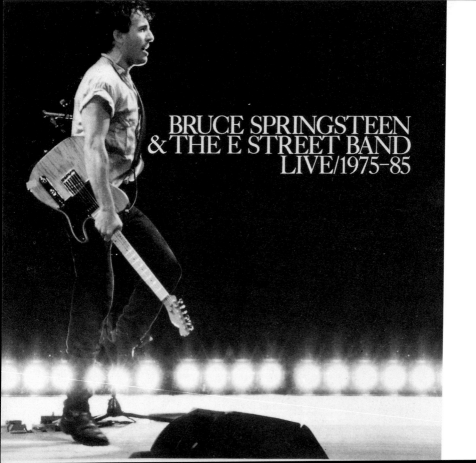

BRUCE SPRINGSTEEN
& THE E STREET BAND
LIVE/1975-85

BRUCE SPRINGSTEEN & THE E. STREET BAND LIVE/1975-85

(COLUMBIA, CBS 4502272; RELEASED: DECEMBER 1986)

After the success of 'Born To Run', as his sets stretched from 90 minutes to three hours plus, Springsteen's reputation had been built on his live shows and fans clamoured for a live souvenir. Landau was now firmly on board, and both he and Bruce were reluctant to commit to a live set. For Springsteen, a live album was simply revisiting familiar territory: "It wasn't ever interesting enough for me. What I was interested in was finding out what kind of songs I could write and finding my way around the studio to get some of the feeling that the band gets on stage…"

There was a boredom factor as well. Ever the perfectionist, Springsteen found the prospect of wading through miles and miles of live tapes, trying to find the definitive version of each song, then sequencing all the selected songs into a showlength package… too much pressure and too much hard work.

Then Landau passed a live four song cassette of 'Born In The USA', 'The River', 'War' and 'Seeds' on to Springsteen, and this alerted both men to the possibilities of a live set. A month later they were dredging through live tapes recorded at concerts over the years, and when they came across the 1975 solo version of 'Thunder Road', both agreed that if there was going to be a comprehensive, live, retrospective Bruce Springsteen set, then this was where it all began.

For too long Springsteen fans had to contend with poor quality bootlegs of those legendary, marathon 75 – 81 concerts. Don't forget, prior to the 1981 'River' tour, Springsteen had only ever played two UK shows – and the first of them, at Hammersmith Odeon, he claimed was one of the worst shows he had ever performed! As word of

Springsteen's legendary lengthy live shows spread across the Atlantic, his European fans were slavering for souvenirs.

Bootlegging is, of course, illegal. The artist and songwriter see none of the money from pirate releases, which steal both financially and artistically from their creator. And yet, and yet… without a doubt, all those who buy Springsteen bootlegs will have everything official in spades anyhow.

Springsteen's special appeal for bootleggers has always been the variety of material available from his live shows. In a professional career of nearly a quarter of a century, he has hardly ever played two shows exactly the same, which whets the appetite of bootleggers and completist fans alike. His notorious perfectionism in the studio sees songs tried and discarded, reworked and rewritten, often many times over before they actually appear on album. Once bootlegged, those fascinating discarded takes are irresistible to curious fans.

Unfortunately, by the time the sprawling three CD 'Live 1975-85' appeared, it was a case of too much, too late. The box seemed designed for those who had only come to Springsteen on the back of his last album –

eight out of 'Born In The USA's' 12 tracks are to be found here, and Springsteen himself was sad that room couldn't be found for 'Glory Days'.

In truth, the live versions of the 'Born In The USA' songs do work much better live than in the studio. 'Cover Me' is transformed from feeble disco pastiche into a taut, muscular rock'n'roll song, while 'Working On The Highway' becomes the storming rock song its studio original only hints at. Other highlights include the hits he gave away ('Because The Night', 'Fire'), the cover versions ('This Land Is Your Land', 'War', 'Jersey Girl') and the full-throated workouts of studio favourites ('Growin' Up', 'Rosalita', 'Badlands' and 'Born To Run').

A better idea would have been double packages of all the facets of Springsteen's concert career. You could have one CD of live versions of album favourites, another of stuff which never made it onto disc at all, but which Springsteen has performed live; and most fans would lap up a whole album of Bruce's cover versions ('Who'll Stop The Rain', 'When You Walk In The Room', 'I Fought The Law', for example). As it was, this lavish package simply endeavoured to achieve the impossible: distil the essence of Bruce Springsteen In Concert onto three CDs.

From such a celebrated live performer and studio perfectionist, there is obviously still plenty more gold to be mined, and a Springsteen box set of unreleased studio material has been on the cards for the past few years.

As it is, 'Live 1975-85' stands as the definitive souvenir of Springsteen as rock'n'roll's premier live performer. The box set soars and dips like a rollercoaster, and while there is undeniably some dead wood on board, it remains a remarkable snapshot of Springsteen in action. The stately, subdued 'Thunder Road' explodes into 'Adam Raised A Cain'. The rap in 'Growin' Up' gives a flavour of Bruce as raconteur, while 'Raise Your Hand' shows what a great bar band the E.Street bunch were. 'Independence Day' demonstrates just how capable Springsteen was at holding an audience spellbound, then 'WHAM!', you're slammed into 'Badlands'.

'Live 1975-85' also finally offers a legitimate opportunity to hear the 'Nebraska' material with The E.Street Band, a subdued and reflective section of the set that runs from 'Racing In The Street', through 'This Land Is Your Land' and 'Nebraska', until Springsteen slams back with 'Born In The USA'.

As a preamble to 'The River' the third CD opens with a spellbinding monologue about Springsteen's experience of his draft medical and the bitter relationship with his father before a long stretch of recent songs ('Darlington County', 'Working On The Highway', 'Cover Me', 'I'm On Fire', 'Bobby Jean', 'My Hometown', 'No Surrender') broken only by 'The Promised Land' and 'Born To Run', before it concludes with Tom Waits' 'Jersey Girl'.

'Live 1975-85' proved to be Springsteen's swansong with The E.Street Band. It marked the end of an era, the end of a particular road, that had begun in the clubs and bars of New Jersey, and which ended on the stages of huge stadiums all around the world.

"We played the live album in my room," Springsteen recalled, "We all sat there and listened to it. And I said 'Well, 10 years, there it is. When you have those little babies, and they want to know what you did these past 10 years, you play them this record'. I think it is something to be proud of."

That pride didn't extend to Springsteen keeping The E.Street Band on the payroll though. In 1989, he made a series of telephone calls which put an end to his band. "It was like being married to someone for 18 years," Clarence Clemons told *Mojo*, "And they say 'I want a divorce' when you think everything is fine."

Full track listing,

CD1: Thunder Road (5.44), Adam Raised A Cain (5.25), Spirit In The Night (6.23), 4th Of July, Asbury Park (Sandy) (6.32), Paradise By The 'C' (3.53), Fire (2.49), Growin' Up (7.56), It's Hard To Be A Saint In The City (4.37), Backstreets (7.33), Rosalita (Come Out Tonight) (10.07), Raise Your Hand (4.57), Hungry Heart (4.29) Two Hearts (3.07);

CD2: Cadillac Ranch (4.51), You Can Look (But You Better Not Touch) (3.56), Independence Day (5.07), Badlands (5.15), Because The Night (5.17), Candy's Room (3.17), Darkness On The Edge Of Town (4.18), Racing In The Street (8.10), This Land Is Your Land (4.19), Nebraska (4.16), Johnny 99 (4.23), Reason To Believe (5.15), Born In The USA (6.08), Seeds (5.14);

CD3: The River (11.40), War (4.51), Darlington County (5.11), Working On The Highway (4.02), The Promised Land (5.34), Cover Me (6.55), I'm On Fire (4.24), Bobby Jean (4.28), My Hometown (5.11), Born To Run (5.01), No Surrender (4.40), Tenth Avenue Freeze-Out (4.19), Jersey Girl (6.30).

The material which constitutes the bulk of 'Live 1975-85' are previously recorded songs, most of them ('Thunder Road' is a notable exception) flexed and extended on the concert platform. They have been discussed in their chronological place on Springsteen's studio albums. Detailed here are the songs which are exclusive to 'Bruce Springsteen & The E.Street Band Live 1975 - 85'.

PARADISE BY THE 'C'

A second-half concert opener during 1978, this instrumental was originally used as the melody of an unreleased 1974 Springsteen song, 'A Love So Fine'. 'Paradise By The C' was pressed up as a promotional 12" single, but never released. A rambunctious R&B style piece, largely included as a showcase for The E.Street Band's instrumental virtuosity

– spotlight again on The Big Man. "That's bar band music," Springsteen told Dave Marsh. "That's who we are… That's what we were doing in those clubs – we were blowin' the roof off with that kinda stuff."

FIRE

Originally recorded for 'Darkness On The Edge Of Town', but as pianist Roy Bittan observed: "Bruce will throw a hit record off an album, as he did when we recorded 'Fire', and everybody agreed 'Fire' was one of the best songs he wrote for that album. But he would not put it on because it's not what he wanted to say on 'Darkness…'".

Springsteen had written the song specifically for Elvis Presley, but the demo only reached Elvis weeks before he died. In his concert monologues that paid tribute to Elvis, Bruce often recalled the night of April 29, 1976, when he clambered over the walls of Graceland: "I said 'Is Elvis here?' (A guard) said, no he was in Lake Tahoe, or something. Well, now I'm pulling all the cheap shots I can think – I was on *Time*, I play guitar, Elvis is my hero, all the things I never say to anybody,

because I figure I've got to get a message through… He thought I was just another crazy fan, which I was."

The Pointer Sisters took the song to No.2 on the US charts in 1978.

RAISE YOUR HAND

An Eddie Floyd song, cut with Booker T & The MGs in 1966. Southern soul was only one of the fiery ingredients in Springsteen's unique musical chowder. This version came from the legendary 1978 Roxy shows, although Bruce had performed the song regularly as an encore during 1976/77. In Memphis in April 1976, Springsteen was joined onstage by Eddie Floyd, and they duetted on Floyd's big hit 'Knock On Wood' as well as 'Raise Your Hand'.

BECAUSE THE NIGHT

Jimmy Iovine had worked with Springsteen, and was also producing Patti Smith's 'Easter' album. Springsteen passed a tape of 'Because The Night' via Iovine to Smith "because he thought it would suit my voice"

Smith told *Mojo* in 1995. "The 'Because The Night' was Bruce's line, the rest was pretty much just humming and mumbling, and then he had the chorus. So the rest of the lyrics were mine." Smith's version was her only hit, reaching UK No.5 in 1978 (US No.13), and she bought her dad a car with the profits. Springsteen's version is taut and sinuous, a regular concert favourite until the mid-Eighties. A studio version was slated for 'Darkness On The Edge Of Town', then 'The River', then it was put on the back burner.

THIS LAND IS YOUR LAND

"One of the most beautiful songs ever written" is how Bruce introduces Woody Guthrie's best known anthem. He had become an enthusiastic Guthrie convert leading up to 'Nebraska' and was particularly impressed by Joe Klein's biography of his hero. Guthrie's song had been written in response to Irving Berlin's 'God Bless America' and Springsteen included the alternative American national anthem at virtually every show during 1980/81. Guthrie's clarion call had become the spearhead of the Sixties folk revival when it was recorded by all the "children of Woody"– Ramblin' Jack Elliott, Pete Seeger, Peter, Paul & Mary, Country Joe McDonald…

SEEDS

Made its début during the European leg of the 'Born In The USA' tour in 1985. Springsteen introduced it: "We were down in Texas… saw a lotta folks down there from the Northeast… who'd moved South looking for work on the oil rigs, in the oil fields. And when they got down there, the price of oil dropped and there wasn't any jobs… You'd see 'em sleeping in tents out on the side of the highway or in their cars at night with nothing to do but move on." Springsteen's lyrics evoke the migrant Okies of John Steinbeck's *Grapes Of Wrath*, victims of an earlier Great Depression.

WAR

Edwin Starr's 1970 US No.1 has one of the great pop opening lines, which Springsteen fully milked. Taken as the first single from the set, it reached US No.8 and UK No.18. The 12" single of 'War' also featured an otherwise unavailable 10-minute live version of 'Incident On 57th Street'.

JERSEY GIRL

Tom Waits wrote 'Jersey Girl' for his wife Kathleen and had included it on his 1980 album 'Heartattack & Vine'. The song was a natural choice for Springsteen and in 1981 he began performing it in concert, later that year Waits joined him onstage in LA for a duet. Springsteen first released the song as the B-side of 'Cover Me', the same version from Meadowlands Arena which concludes 'Live 1975-85'. Originally, the plan had been to wrap the set up with the penultimate 'Tenth Avenue Freeze-Out' ("the cast of characters and friends; it's the band"), but Landau felt something more subdued would provide a more dignified conclusion. Springsteen concurred: "That's the same guy that's on the boardwalk in 'Sandy', back in the same place. The same guy in 'Rosalita' – you know, he got that Jersey girl."

BRUCE SPRINGSTEEN

TUNNEL OF LOVE

TUNNEL OF LOVE

(COLUMBIA COL 4602702; RELEASED: OCTOBER 1987)

Long before it was announced that his marriage to model Julianne Phillips had broken up, Springsteen fans knew, just by listening to 'Tunnel Of Love'. It was not the album of a man made buoyant by his recent marriage.

Springsteen first met the first Mrs Springsteen in October 1984, while he was still touring to promote 'Born In The USA'. Michael Jackson aside, he was the biggest rock star on the planet. Julianne Phillips was a $2,000 a day model, who came from a closely-knit, comfortably middle class family in Portland, Oregon.

They were married in May 1985, at the epicentre of a media hurricane. On the surface, the two had precious little in common: in her profession looking after herself was a prerequisite, which meant lengthy and exhausting work-outs and a carefully balanced diet. Although no longer a junk-food junkie, Springsteen's diet was still the despair of anyone vaguely health-conscious. His work-outs took the shape of three or four hour concerts. Julianne was 10 years Springsteen's junior and her hobbies didn't include hanging out in smoky clubs and bars in Asbury Park while her husband jammed on old rock'n'roll favourites which were hits before she was born.

Bruce-watchers had eyes on stalks when 'Tunnel Of Love' was announced. For once, the Springsteen network had precious little advance information about the forthcoming album. There were rumours that it was a Country & Western collection, largely because some aborted sessions in Los Angeles had featured Chris Hillman's New Rose Band. The 1986 sessions then switched to New York, but Springsteen was clearly unhappy with both the location and the proposed album's overall sound, so everything was switched again, this time to his home studio. "Security was extraordinarily tight," announced *Backstreets*' Charles R. Cross.

'Tunnel Of Love' was remarkable for another reason, inasmuch as Springsteen had very little material left over from the sessions – only two songs ('Lucky Man' and 'Two For The Road') appeared subsequently as B-sides, which suggested a lack of inspiration, although Springsteen himself was confident about its intentions: "The record was made very quickly, in two or three weeks. It was a very peaceful working process and the record was intimate. I wanted the record to be non-mythic, just real… not austere, clean, arranged. I worked six hours a day and the songs came pretty easy."

It was kept firmly under wraps, being recorded largely at the couple's new home in Rumsom, New Jersey. This would be Bruce's first album since his marriage and everyone was expecting a sloppy, sentimental collection, a pot of gloop aimed right at Mrs Springsteen.

What they got was an album about as sloppy and romantic as an Ingmar Bergman film. Not as stark as 'Nebraska', 'Tunnel Of Love' nevertheless featured a stripped-down E.Street Band

and songs which came straight out of the emotional badlands. Having made the commitment to marry, Springsteen was allegedly bitterly disappointed when his wife refused to give up her modelling career and concentrate on raising a family. Cracks began to appear in the marriage façade from early on, and Springsteen's bitterness was evident on almost every track on this latest album. He spoke of writing "love songs in a way that had not been done… that way before" and 'Tunnel Of Love' certainly reflected that; but as an album from a recently married man, it was as emotionally turbulent as a rollercoaster at sea. All the credit his wife received was a "Thanks Juli" at the end of the credits.

'Tunnel Of Love' dealt with hypocrisy and betrayal, love mislaid and love lost. It did not make for comfortable listening. While 'Nebraska' had focused on broader issues, this was a report from the front line of the marriage wars.

"'Born In The USA' was the best kind of thoughtful, tough, mainstream rock 'n' roll record, but… it was misinterpreted and oversimplified by listeners looking for slogans rather than ideas," wrote Steve Pond in *Rolling Stone* in his 'Tunnel Of Love' review. "The five record

live set that followed the tour was a suitably oversize way to sum up Bruce Springsteen, the Boss, American rock icon. But where do you go from there? Trying to top 'Born In The USA' with another collection of rock anthems would have been foolhardy artistically; on the other hand, to react the way Springsteen did after the breakthrough 1980 success of 'The River' – with a home made record as stark and forbidding as 'Nebraska' – would have turned an inspired gesture into a formula. So 'Tunnel Of Love' walks a middle ground…"

'Tunnel Of Love' was a conscious attempt at scaling down the hysteria which had surrounded Springsteen since the release of 'Born In the USA' three years before. In his mind, he was already planning a different type of music, one which reflected his new-found intimacy, which perforce had meant bidding The E.Street Band "au revoir".

The finished album was effectively a Bruce Springsteen solo record, the sleeve reminded you just who The E.Street Band are, but they appear nowhere together on the record, with just odd members appearing on odd tracks, and not a note of Clarence Clemons' trademark saxophone to be found anywhere.

"When I wrote the record I wanted to write a different type of romantic song, one that I felt took in the different types of emotional experience of any real relationship," Springsteen told *Rolling Stone* soon after its release. "I guess I wanted to make a record about what I felt. Really letting another person into your life, that's a frightening thing. That's something that's filled with shadows and doubts, and also wonderful things and beautiful things, things that you cannot experience alone…

"I suppose it doesn't have the physical reach out and grab you by the throat and thrash you around of, say, 'Born In The USA'. 'Tunnel Of Love' is a rock record, but most of the stuff is mid-tempo, and it's more rhythm oriented, very different. It was more meticulously arranged than anything I've done since 'Born To Run'."

Recorded at home in New Jersey in almost monk-like seclusion, 'Tunnel Of Love' was cut in Springsteen's tiny studio where there was no air-conditioning, and if a passing car sounded its horn, it made its way onto tape, and the song had to be re-done. Musically, it was Springsteen stripped down. Far removed from the high energy of 'Born To Run' and the bombast of 'Born In The USA', 'Tunnel Of Love' signalled a sea change in Springsteen's music. It would be his last album for five years and was a decidedly low-key swansong.

"The way you counteract the size (of stardom) is by becoming more intimate in your work. And I suppose that's why after I did 'Born In The USA', I made an intimate record... a record that was really addressed to my core audience, my longtime fans."

AIN'T GOT YOU

Opening a capella, this light-hearted, rhythm based song is deceptive. For a man as recently married as Springsteen, the first song on an album whose chorus ran: "The only thing I ain't got, baby, I ain't got you" sounded warning bells. Otherwise, it's a nicely tongue-in-cheek look at the sort of fame which had winged Springsteen's way following his endless MTV rotation from 1984 thru' 1986. The first Bruce song to make mention of caviar.

TOUGHER THAN THE REST

Wistful and contemplative, 'Tougher Than The Rest' marks out the territory covered by the whole of 'Tunnel Of Love'. It's a song which echoes the album's cover photo, dark and brooding. There is a menacing edge to Springsteen's performance: for almost the first time on record, he doesn't sound like he wants to be liked – even the serial killer on 'Nebraska' had aroused some sympathy. Here he swaggers and boasts, a cocksure "sweet-talkin' Romeo". 'Tougher Than The Rest' was the third single lifted from the album, and in the UK, where it reached No.13, it was the biggest hit.

The 12" single included a six-minute live version from a Los Angeles concert. 'Tougher Than The Rest' was later covered by Emmylou Harris on her 'Brand New Dance' album. It cropped up again in 1992 when Everything But The Girl included it on their 'Covers' EP.

ALL THAT HEAVEN WILL ALLOW

The 1955 movie *All That Heaven Allows* was an old-fashioned tearjerker starring Rock Hudson and Jane Wyman, in which upperclass woman falls in love with son-of-the-soil gardener. Bruce takes note and writes song? Covered by Cuban-American, country rock band The Mavericks on their wonderful second album, 'What A Crying Shame' (1994), a version which received the thumbs-up from Springsteen himself.

SPARE PARTS

Released to coincide with Springsteen's Tunnel Of Love European Tour, 'Spare Parts' reached UK No.32 a year after the album's release. A heartfelt vocal, narrative and arrangement which wouldn't have sounded out of place on 'Nebraska'. Springsteen's blistering guitar matches the mood. A bitter and clinically cold tale, in which a moment of passionate penetration scars the life of the illegitimate baby's mother. It ends with dreams and future plans pawned for "some good cold cash". The 12" single includes a live version of the song recorded at Sheffield.

CAUTIOUS MAN

Even more than 'Spare Parts', 'Cautious Man' would have sat quite happily on the sparse and solo 'Nebraska'; like that album's 'Mansion On The Hill', this song acknowledges a debt to Robert Mitchum's sinister preacher in Charles Laughton's 1955 masterpiece *The Night Of The Hunter*. Mitchum's Harry Powell had 'Love' and 'Hate' tattooed on opposite hands, and his graphic battle between good and evil finds echo on 'Cautious Man', where Springsteen's Bill Horton sports 'Love' and 'Fear'. Bruce on guitar and atmospheric keyboards evokes dark and lonely landscapes. Slowly and hypnotically, he builds up a cinematic depiction of a marriage built on uncertainty, which even in the freshness of married bliss, is already crumbling. Again, you found yourself wondering whether the line "he knew in a restless heart the seed of betrayal lay" was the sort of emotion which a recently married man should be confessing.

WALK LIKE A MAN

Languorous and autobiographical tale, Bruce on the eve of his own marriage reflects how his father coped, and finally begins to comprehend about adulthood. A bit late in the day some say, but the album's heartfelt tribute from Bruce to Douglas, kid to dad, is nevertheless touching. "I remember the night that I got married. I was standing by myself, and I was waiting for my wife, and I can remember standing there thinking 'Man, I have everything. I got it all'."

TUNNEL OF LOVE

Bruce goes back to the circus for the first time since 'Wild Billy's Circus Story' on his second album. Using the fairground ride as a metaphor for marriage, the album's title track comes

nearest to the 'old' Bruce Springsteen, with half The E.Street Band playing on the track. Again, you wonder how Julianne Springsteen reacted to a line like "It's easy for two people to lose each other in this Tunnel Of Love". Upbeat tempo, but in tone reminiscent of Robert Lowell's lines: "If we see light at the end of the tunnel, it's the light of the oncoming train". 'Tunnel Of Love' was the album's second single, UK No.45, US No.9.

TWO FACES

Hypocrisy and deceit lie close to the surface here. Cheesy fairground organ at the close is reminiscent of Del Shannon's 'Runaway', but otherwise 'Two Faces' is standard 'Tunnel Of Love' material: mid-paced tune, but with Bruce sounding funereal, torn both ways, neither of them a winner. And all the while, "dark clouds come rolling by".

BRILLIANT DISGUISE

The album's lead-off single, a UK No.20 and US No.5, which suggested that the subsequent 'Tunnel Of Love' album would be a lot lighter than it eventually ended up. Of the song, Bruce wrote "After '85 I'd had enough and turned inward to write about men, women and love, things that had previously been on the periphery of my work." These were certainly songs that were coming from some dark place, much of the 'Tunnel Of Love' material dealt with the masks we wear, and the bitter realisation of what lies behind the masks.

ONE STEP UP

The natural desire is to move forward, but it is often overruled by the emotional tug which pulls you inexorably back. Just as, buried beneath the Fab harmonies, 'Help!' was a John Lennon cry from the heart, so 'One Step Up' comes from Springsteen's emotional heartland. Like so many of the 'Tunnel Of Love' songs, this one is set in or around a cold, empty house, which is soon vacated for highway – except that in this case, the car won't even start. Springsteen characterises the state of this relationship as "another battle in our dirty little war". The irony, of course, is that the haunting echo vocal is provided by the future second Mrs Springsteen. 'One Step

Up' was an American-only single, where it reached No.13 in March 1988. Beautifully covered by Clive Gregson & Christine Collister on 'Love Is A Strange Hotel' in 1990.

WHEN YOU'RE ALONE

The title says it all. Springsteen admitted: "My relationships always ended poorly. I didn't really know how to have a relationship with a woman."

VALENTINE'S DAY

Behind the clouds which engulf 'Tunnel Of Love' can sometimes be glimpsed a faint ray of sunshine, and if it's really there, it is the hope of parenthood which provides the light. 'Valentine's Day' begins alone and in the dark, in the second verse there is a promise of fatherhood and a brief glimmer of light, but overall there is an air of quiet desperation in the album's final song. Mournful and waltz-like, the melody is made all the more melancholy by Springsteen's dour vocal and the prospect of a "lonely Valentine". Fade to black…

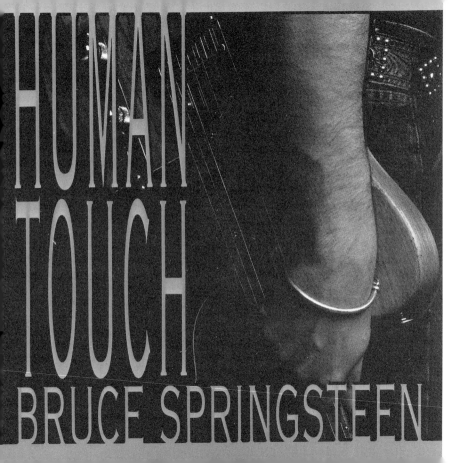

HUMAN TOUCH

BRUCE SPRINGSTEEN

HUMAN TOUCH & LUCKY TOWN

(COLUMBIA, COL 4714232 & COLUMBIA, COL 4714242 RESPECTIVELY; BOTH RELEASED: MARCH 1992)

In rock'n'roll, an artist's career is flagged by album releases. Their development, or lack of it, is signposted by studio projects – live albums and Greatest Hits compilations are seen simply as treading water. Bruce Springsteen had taken a three-year absence between 'Born To Run' and 'Darkness On The Edge Of Town'; the delay between 'Tunnel Of Love' and 'Human Touch'/'Lucky Town' was nearer to five years.

During his time away from the studio, Springsteen had not been idle. He had undertaken a 1988 world tour to promote Amnesty International, appeared at charity concerts, contributed to charity and tribute albums and paid his respects at memorial concerts for John Hammond and Harry Chapin. He had turned 40, and was widely seen sporting the sort of goatee last seen in Hollywood movies about Parisian Bohemians.

Springsteen had also undertaken a blitz of bar-hopping appearances, matching his 1982 frenzy of popping up unannounced. This has always been one of Bruce's most endearing habits: even at the height of his fame, he was as

likely to turn up and play in a smoky New Jersey bar as he was to appear headlining at some enormous, anonymous stadium.

Asbury Park's Stone Pony was the Springsteen fan's equivalent to The Beatles' Cavern Club. The Stone Pony was where Bruce would drop in to jam with local band Cats On A Smooth Surface, whiling the night away with a selection of rock'n'roll oldies. What was so engaging and mesmerising about these spontaneous jams was the commitment Springsteen brought to the shows: he treated every gig like it was top of the bill at the Hollywood Bowl.

From May 1982, right up until the massive 'Born In The USA' tour of mid-1984, Springsteen's unannounced guest slots had constituted a virtual club tour in themselves. It had been an opportunity to let off steam on such time-honoured favourites as 'Twist & Shout', 'Summertime Blues', 'Long Tall Sally', 'Around And Around'. Springsteen also used these club dates to try out new songs: 'On The Prowl' and 'From Small Things, Big Things One Day Come' – which he performed alongside Dave Edmunds who later recorded the song.

Seven years on, Springsteen's surprise appearances were all the more remarkable, given his post-'Born In The USA' superstar status. The club dates were not just a cynical opportunity to see how new songs would work in front of a crowd, Springsteen genuinely got off on the whites-of-their eyeballs approach. While mega-bands like The Rolling Stones would later make a big thing about playing a 'surprise' club date in every town their stadium size carnival lumbered through, Bruce Springsteen just got down and got on with it.

In October 1987, Springsteen had sung Bob Dylan's 'Forever Young' at a memorial service for Columbia Records' John Hammond. A fortnight later, he jammed with the high school band opposite where he lived

in New Jersey. In December, he performed at a tribute concert to the late Harry Chapin (see final chapter) and a week later, joined Paul Simon, Billy Joel and Lou Reed to sing Dion's 'Teenager In Love' at a charity concert at Madison Square Garden which Simon had instigated to benefit the city's homeless.

The 1988 Tunnel Of Love tour saw Springsteen radically alter his stage show – eight of the intimate 'Tunnel Of Love' songs became an integral part of the set, while a number of long-time favourites were abandoned. 'Born To Run' was regularly featured in its stark, solo version and a full-time touring four-man horn section emphasised the punchier, R&B nature of the shows.

Springsteen's smallest audience on the tour was in Rome, when at three in the morning he was strolling with Patti Scialfa, and passed some hippies on the Spanish Steps. Borrowing an acoustic guitar, Bruce ran through 'I'm On Fire' and 'The River', then moved on.

With Reagan coming to the end of the second term of his Presidency and former CIA head George Bush waiting in the wings, Springsteen hadn't lightened up much since

'Nebraska', six years before: "That sense of dread, man, it's everywhere," he told *Rolling Stone* at the onset of the tour. "It's outside, it's inside, it's in the bedroom, it's on the street. The main thing was to show people striving for that idea of home: people forced out of their homes, people looking for homes, people trying to build their homes, people looking for shelter, for comfort, for tenderness, a little bit of kindness somewhere."

Springsteen was angry at the way he saw the government of his country disenfranchising many of its citizens. On finding a note from Oliver North's secretary Fawn Hall, requesting a meeting, Springsteen responded in one of his finest offstage moments: "I don't like you. I don't like your boss. I don't like what you did. Thank you."

While still on tour, the press was full of the news that Julianne Springsteen was filing for divorce. In June 1988, *The Sun* gleefully published "The pictures that will cost The Boss £75 million", showing Springsteen kissing backing singer Patti Scialfa.

Patti had joined The E.Street Band for the 'Born In The USA' tour in 1984. A real-life Jersey Girl, she was born in 1953 in Long Branch, New Jersey, and was well known around the Jersey music scene. Prior to working with Springsteen, Patti had appeared on records by Narada Michael Walden and Southside Johnny.

Even with his marriage in tatters and the tabloids stalking his every step, Springsteen still committed to Amnesty International's Human Rights Now! tour late in 1988, appearing with Sting, Peter Gabriel, Tracy Chapman and Youssou N'Dour, and playing places never before visited by rock bands – Zimbabwe, Chile, Hungary and India.

Springsteen's Amnesty set was effectively a Greatest Hits package ('Born In The USA', 'The River', 'Thunder Road' and the electric 'Born To Run'). A highlight of the Springsteen set was his cover of Bob Dylan's 'Chimes Of Freedom' (see final chapter), which along with Bob Marley's 'Get Up, Stand Up', became the anthem of Human Rights Now!

As the Amnesty tour concluded in October, Springsteen disappeared with Patti, but by the middle of 1989, he was hot to trot. Every week over the summer, he popped up at clubs around New Jersey blasting out old-time rock'n'roll with local bands. His only official

Pissed off as he was at the state of the nation, Springsteen was nowhere near as cheesed off as The E.Street Band, who were summarily dismissed after nearly 20 years together. Bruce and Patti married on June 8, 1991, following the birth of their first child, Evan James on July 25, 1990. A daughter, Jessica Rae followed on December 30, 1991.

Rumours abounded of a new record, but with his new family as his first priority, Springsteen was cautious. The rumours were given substance in November 1990, when at a charity show in Los Angeles for civil rights organisation the Christic Institute Springsteen made his first announced concert appearance since the Amnesty tour of two years before.

Sprinkled among the hits ('Darkness On The Edge Of Town', 'Thunder Road') at these two solo shows, were some intriguing returns to neglected glories ('Wild Billy's Circus Story', 'Mansion On The Hill') and three songs which were to appear on the next Springsteen release(s). Early in 1992, the rumours became hard fact when in a surprise move, it was announced that not one – but count 'em – two new Springsteen albums were ready for release.

Springsteen knew by now that he could

appearances on record were on a tribute album to Woody Guthrie and Leadbelly, and on a UK charity compilation of Presley covers, 'The Last Temptation Of Elvis' (see final chapter).

never again reach the mass audience which had grown up around him with 'Born In The USA'. It was almost as if he was intent on defusing his own myth, something which these albums went a long way towards doing. For someone whose career up until 1986 had been a map of how to do it, Springsteen badly miscalculated with these two albums: released together on the same day, but as full price separates.

He may have lost sales on 'Human Touch' and 'Lucky Town', but he hadn't lost his sense of humour. Only weeks after their release, Springsteen could be heard on American radio joking: "In the crystal ball, I see romance, I see adventure, I see financial reward. I see those albums, man, I see them going back up the charts. I see them rising past that old Def Leppard, past that Kriss Kross. I see them all the way up past 'Weird' Al Yankovic... Wait a minute. We're slipping. We're slipping down the charts. We're going down, down, out of sight, into the darkness..."

The official story goes that one further track was needed to complete the 'Human Touch' album, which was scheduled for a Spring 1991 release. But Springsteen was on

a roll, and when Jon Landau heard 'Living Proof', he told his boy to keep at it. Over a six week period, Springsteen came up with a further nine new songs, which both men felt constituted another ready-made new album.

"By the time I finished the album," Springsteen told Robert Hilburn, "I was at a different place in my life. I was a father and having this uplifting and happy relationship. I felt revitalized, and I didn't feel that was reflected in the 'Human Touch' album.

"I didn't hear the 'Hallelujah, raise your hands to the sky (spirit), of someone who felt as thankful and as blessed as I did. I had been away a long time, and I could imagine people asking 'What's happened... where are you nowadays?' I also felt like I hadn't risked enough artistically. So I put the record aside and sat with it two or three months. I felt I needed one more song.

Controversy was sparked by the release of both albums simultaneously; Springsteen seemed to be aping Guns n' Roses. Talking to Landau in Stockholm in 1992, I put it to him that Bruce was no stranger to double albums: "It just wasn't a double album to us. It wasn't a serious thought once we had the 'Lucky Town' album...

To us they are very distinct – there's no song you could take from 'Human Touch' and put it on 'Lucky Town', and vice versa, which would flow and feel coherent in that context."

Fans were bitter and vocal in denouncing the paucity of original ideas and inspiration, particularly on 'Human Touch', which probably stands as the weakest album Bruce Springsteen has ever lent his name to. This was moribund, muscle-bound rock'n'roll. 'Soul Driver', 'Real World' and 'Man's Job' were empty and soul-less. Springsteen sounded like he lacked real inspiration, and was – for the first time in his career – padding an album with sub-standard material.

'Lucky Town' was an altogether more appealing package, right down to the cover, where Bruce clearly modelled himself on Pogue Shane MacGowan. It was completed in a six-week spurt, but still left Springsteen fans clutching at straws. For Springsteen, it was an adult album, the themes of parenthood dominating and it was good to hear him writing about life as a 40-year-old with one failed marriage behind him, rather than as the eternal teenager in love. After the pleasure his music had brought to so many, no one could deny

Springsteen the opportunity to enjoy fatherhood, but many fans secretly wished that more of the energy he set aside for nappy-changing could be channelled into his music.

For Bruce Springsteen, rock'n'roll had always been the Holy Grail, the deliverance; it had been his salvation as a teenager. As he hit 40, he had followed rock'n'roll into a dead-end, but he survived and on his first record since his remarriage, Springsteen's beloved rock'n'roll took a back seat to the baby buggy. Try as he might to convey and reflect turmoil, this is the album of a contented husband and father.

1) HUMAN TOUCH

HUMAN TOUCH

Slow and reflective, 'Human Touch' could have sat happily on 'Tunnel Of Love'. Autobiographical, Springsteen reflects on his failures, and appears to come to terms with where he is, and who he is. For all the myth-making and public perception of Springsteen as 'The Boss', it is a role he has always denied, perceiving himself in far less mythic terms.

Here he sings that he's nobody's bargain "But hell, a little touch up and a little paint…"

SOUL DRIVER

The song displays a promising start lyrically, set in the smoky swamp of The Rolling Stones' bayoux, *circa* 'Sticky Fingers', but it's otherwise unremarkable. Bruce's harmonies with soul giant Sam Moore are somewhere lost in the flood.

57 CHANNELS (AND NOTHIN' ON)

A worthy, bass-heavy addition to the Boss canon. Live, they turned the amps up to No. 11, and prefaced Bruce's song by playing a tape of Jimi Hendrix's apocalyptic reworking of 'The Star-Spangled Banner'. '57 Channels…' crackled with pent-up frustration and caught some of the Los Angeles nervousness following the 1992 riots. It is also only the second song in which Springsteen invokes the sacred name of the King of rock'n'roll - 'Johnny Bye Bye' being the first. It's "in the blessed name of Elvis" that he blasts the TV into 57 pieces. Fun.

CROSS MY HEART

Slow, monotonous rockabilly number which testifies to Springsteen's claim that he tried to write songs in different styles for this album. But whereas when he had done it before – whether Elvis-style rock'n'roll on 'Fire', or narrative folk ballad with 'Nebraska' – he did it from the heart, now it just came across as a technical exercise. Just one of the empty numbers which fill up 'Human Touch'.

GLORIA'S EYES

Bruce trying to sound like the Bruce of old. Muscle-flexing rocker. File somewhere between 'Crush On You' and 'Out On The Street'. Maybe subconsciously Bruce tries to invoke Van Morrison's 'Gloria'. Maybe not…

WITH EVERY WISH

"(It's about) growing up and realising what a life with consequences is all about. When you're a kid, you have a dream and the way you imagine it is really a life without complications. When you get older, the trickiest thing is not to give in to cynicism, and you get to an age… where you don't have the time to spare. You have to understand the limitations of your own life and keep pushing through it. That's what 'With Every Wish' is about, keeping on moving forward," Springsteen told *Q*'s David Hepworth.

Melodically similar to Paul Simon's 'Hearts & Bones', lyrically it's back to the bayoux. Mark Isham's trumpet strikes a discordant note, an accordion would have amplified the song's cajun-style story. The song's refrain finds echo in the question at the heart of 'The River', except that this time around the warning is emphatic: "With every wish there comes a curse."

ROLL OF THE DICE

Pianist Roy Bittan was the only ex-E.Street Band member Springsteen used on either of these albums (apart from Patti and organist David Sancious, back after nearly 20 years). It was Bittan who supplied the melody, and Bruce: "Went home and wrote the song. It was really about what I was trying to do: I was trying to get up the nerve to take a chance." 'Roll Of The Dice' is a full-throated, epic, E.Street Band type song, with Bittan's piano well to the fore. The most 'Bruce' sounding song on the album,

you could even imagine this one slotting comfortably on to 'Born In The USA'.

REAL WORLD

A duet with Sam Moore again, which at least gives the soul man something to sing about. Otherwise, little to write home about: Bruce rhymes "world" with "flags unfurled", mentions "tumbling dice" – arguably greatest-ever Rolling Stones single – and on to fade away.

ALL OR NOTHIN' AT ALL

See 'Gloria's Eyes'. Punchy rocker, helped along by Bruce's gutsy guitar. What makes this such a dispiriting listening experience, is that as so often on these two records, when Bruce rocks out he sounds like bargain-basement Z Z Top. And this from the man who gave the world 'Born To Run'.

MAN'S JOB

Embarrassing testosterone rocker. The sort of thing Bruce could have got away with 20 years before; but hearing a man revelling in father-

hood as he muscles up to middle age, singing
with all the clumsiness of a teenager is plain
old-fashioned and long past its sell-by date.
See 'Gloria's Eyes'.

I WISH I WERE BLIND

'I Wish I Were Blind' is a pensive duet with former Righteous Brother Bobby Hatfield, which
with a little rearranging, could have fitted into
'Nebraska', such is the bleak note struck by

Springsteen. "It's about that sinking feeling," Springsteen told *Q*'s David Hepworth. "There's a world of love, a world of beauty, a world of fear and a world of loss and they are the same world, and that person is wending his way through the maze and at that moment he's very in touch with… those things. That song gets that picture." Biblical, bitter and twisted, it is an atmospheric song, that ebbs away with a scorching Springsteen guitar solo.

THE LONG GOODBYE

The best out and out rocker on the album, with a chorus that swings like a jackhammer. Springsteen filches the title from Raymond Chandler's classic private eye novel, but little else. Popular live favourite, maybe because this is the new Boss, same as the old Boss.

REAL MAN

A Saturday night at the movies song, refreshingly tongue in cheek. David Sancious' organ manages to replicate the sound of a brass section. 'Real man' is a mocking and an entertaining enough throwaway, but to have a

43-year-old man expressing the emotions of a 16-year-old is still a mistake.

PONY BOY

Overt sentimentality from father to child is rare in rock'n'roll – David Bowie got away with it on 'Kooks', Bob Dylan with 'Forever Young' and Paul Simon on 'St Judy's Comet'. Bruce remembered his grandmother singing this to him as a baby, and 40 years on, found it was the one song guaranteed to send Evan James quietly to sleep. Joined on harmony vocals by his firstborn's mother, 'Pony Boy' is beguiling and quietly charming, it is nevertheless an odd ending to a strange album.

2) LUCKY TOWN

BETTER DAYS

"With a young son and about to get married (for the last time) I was feelin' like a happy guy who has his rough days rather than vice versa." Brash and crashing opener, it demands that you sit up and listen. 'Better Days' is the best song from the whole bunch, maybe because it reminded fans of former glories. Springsteen is speaking with the mature voice of an adult but performing with the enthusiasm of a teenager. Bruce swaggers through the song and hikes it right up to glory on the third verse as he sings: "Tonight this fool's halfway to heaven and just a mile outta hell…".

LUCKY TOWN

Hypnotic and quietly compelling song, which immediately suggests that there is more substance here than on Human Touch. It's a song about rebirth and the realisation that, hey, life does have something to offer even to a jaded old superstar like Bruce Springsteen.

LOCAL HERO

"The first verse of the song is completely true," Springsteen told Q's David Hepworth, "I was driving through a town I grew up in and I looked over and there was a five and ten cent store with a black velvet painting of Bruce Lee, a picture of me on 'Born In The USA' and a picture of a dog next to me! I said Wow, I gotta get a photo of that! It was on sale for $19.99." One of Springsteen's most engaging songs, a tongue-in-cheek look at his own celebrity. Nice harmonica too.

IF I SHOULD FALL BEHIND

Intimate and touching love song. Springsteen's warm vocal lends the song an immediacy and leaves little doubt who the sentiments are directed toward. A reflective and poignant song, about a couple on the eve of their wedding, the final verse has a directness and honesty which makes it undeniably one of Springsteen's most heartfelt and affecting love songs. Its strength lies in its directness and simplicity.

LEAP OF FAITH

Bruce gets horny ("Now your legs were heaven and your breasts were the altar…"). A testament to the second Mrs Springsteen, one from the heart, of the kind which the first Mrs Springsteen missed out on in 'Tunnel Of Love'. Carnality is an equal part of real love here, but ultimately, Bruce is "born again" by Patti's love.

THE BIG MUDDY

Brooding, bluesy swamp-rock, with a keening guitar and a pining vocal. The song is a return to the territory Springsteen stalked on 'Nebraska', detailed and observational. Inspired by the short stories of Flannery O'Connor, and – on 'The Big Muddy' – Pete Dexter, from whose *Paris, Trout* he quotes in the song.

LIVING PROOF

'Living Proof' delivered the bellicosity and pounding power which all the flexing of 'Soul Man' on the other album had failed to muster. Inspired by listening to Bob Dylan's triple CD retrospective of 1991, 'The Bootleg Series', Bruce was particularly affected by 'Series Of Dreams', which directly inspired 'Living Proof',

his testament to his son Evan James. "I realised that here was one of the biggest experiences of my life," Springsteen told Robert Hilburn, "and I felt like 'I'm hiding something'. I hadn't written anything about it. But suddenly I wanted to talk about all I felt… the way you walk through the fear to find the love."

BOOK OF DREAMS

Face pressed against the window, recalling 'My Father's House' from 'Nebraska', Bruce watches the girl of his dream pirouette, he is a voyeur, outside the closeness of family. But by the third verse, 'Book Of Dreams' is back on familiar 'Lucky Town' territory – a couple on the eve of their wedding, with Bruce reflecting on his newfound contentment and the happiness to come.

SOULS OF THE DEPARTED

Watching the news from the Gulf War on CNN, being in LA as the city exploded in the aftermath of the Rodney King verdict… It all makes new father Bruce reflect on just what sort of world his boy is being born into. The song can be linked to 'Wreck On The Highway' on 'The River' – cool and objective until the last verse, when the realisation dawns that that dead seven-year-old kid from East Compton could be the singer's own. "We have left our children a legacy of dread," Springsteen told Robert Hilburn just after the album's release. "That's what being born in the USA is all about now, and it is not going to go away until we address the problems we face as a society."

MY BEAUTIFUL REWARD

A country-styled mid-paced ballad, the album's final track is a song that seems at odds with the contentment displayed so prominently elsewhere on the album. The over-riding image in the song is of the singer stalking a silent, empty mansion, which again recalls the stark and bleak territory of 'Nebraska'. "I really did stumble across it," Bruce told NME's Gavin Martin. "I had the title and I thought 'Great, I'll write this song about what a happy guy I am now'. But it came out the way it came out. It's… about that part of you that's always… isolated is not the right word – but there's a part of you that remains individual, alone or even selfish, no matter how great your relationships or your family life is."

IN CONCERT/MTV PLUGGED

(COLUMBIA, 4738602, RELEASED: MARCH 1993)

MTV's *Unplugged* had begun in low-key fashion in 1989, with Squeeze's Chris Difford & Glenn Tilbrook joining ex-Car Elliot Easton and singer-songwriters Syd Straw and Jules Shear for an acoustic evening. Early Unplugees included Neil Young, Don Henley, Elton John, Black Crowes and The Cure; but it was in 1991, when Paul McCartney and R.E.M. were persuaded to flick the switch 'off' that the show gained its credibility.

Unplugged had provided Rod Stewart and Eric Clapton with artistic rebirths – with Clapton's 'Unplugged' album becoming the biggest-selling of his entire career. Nirvana's 'Unplugged' had been a dignified swan-song to the group's career and Bob Dylan's had offered critics a further opportunity not to write the old groaner off.

Bruce Springsteen was the obvious next choice for MTV. Springsteen's music seemed particularly appropriate to the *Unplugged* format – highlights of his 1980/81 shows were solo acoustic versions of 'This Land Is Your Land', 'Can't Help Falling In Love' and 'Johnny Bye Bye'. 'Nebraska' had displayed Springsteen at his acoustic best, and his solo Christic Institute shows were among the most warmly-received of his recent career. Even during his 1992/93 European tour, highlights included solo, acoustic readings of 'This Hard Land' and 'Satan's Jewel Crown'.

But Bruce wrong-footed 'em all with this heavy-handed souvenir. Inexplicably, Springsteen chose to play the set with his touring band rather than solo and acoustic. 'Plugged', a European-only album, released to coincide with his tour dates, remains Springsteen's biggest miscalculation to date.

Springsteen's 'Plugged' was made doubly disappointing by the fact that – incredibly – it marked only his second-ever live TV appearance, and neither had featured The E.Street Band. Talking to *Musician*'s Bill Flanagan late in 1992, Springsteen had even admitted: "At some point, I want to do an acoustic tour by myself and play in theatres. It's something that I've been wanting to do for a long time."

Unplugged producer Alex Coletti told David Cavanagh of *Q* that MTV had bent the rules because of who they were dealing with: "When you have the chance to work with Bruce Springsteen, he can do what he wants. It was a fantastic show, and it still had a lot of *Unplugged*'s feel. It was very small, very intimate, very loose – and that's all part of what makes *Unplugged* special. But it was very loud!"

The album displayed a laziness, as if Springsteen couldn't be bothered to rehearse a solo or acoustic set, and instead trundled through 90 minutes' worth of highlights from his current tour. But given the agonising which had accompanied the release of his first Live set, 'Plugged' was a spectacularly half-hearted souvenir.

There was also a tawdriness – the back cover simply a plug for the upcoming tour dates – which was uncharacteristic of Springsteen; indeed it seemed as though the whole album was designed to re-promote his poor-selling albums of 1992 – eight of 'Plugged's 13 tracks were taken from 'Human Touch' and 'Lucky Town'.

There was a full-throated revisit to 'Darkness On The Edge Of Town' and a soulful, almost solo 'Thunder Road', which would have been a welcome rarity, had it not been so similar to the version which opened 'Live 1975-85'. 'Atlantic City' made its welcome début on a live album and demonstrated just what a band version of the acoustic 'Nebraska' album might have sounded like, the song benefiting particularly from Roy Bittan's pounding piano.

The real selling-point for fans though, was the inclusion of two otherwise unavailable Springsteen songs: 'Red Headed Woman' and 'Light Of Day'. Otherwise, thin-pickings here for Boss fans.

Full track listing: Red Headed Woman (2.51), Better Days (4.27), Atlantic City (5.38), Darkness On The Edge Of Town (4.40), Man's Job (5.43), Human Touch (7.30), Lucky Town (5.08), I Wish I Were Blind (5.14), Thunder Road (5.29), Light Of Day (8.17), If I Should Fall Behind (4.44), Living Proof (6.05), My Beautiful Reward (5.58)

RED HEADED WOMAN

The album opens promisingly enough, with this solo, acoustic tribute, as Bruce adopts a high, lonesome Jimmie Rodgers-style 'Blue Yodel'. Bruce has fun with the song, relishing the lewd automotive imagery. A touching tribute to the charms of the titian-haired Mrs Springsteen, but really, on repeated listening 'Red Headed Woman' did few favours to anyone besides the in-laws.

LIGHT OF DAY

Screenwriter Paul Schrader (*Taxi Driver, Raging Bull*) had submitted a film script to Springsteen. Bruce declined the role, as he had declined the Marlon Brando role in a musical remake of *The Wild One*, but he liked the title of Schrader's script about a struggling Cleveland bar band – *Born In The USA*. Bruce kept the title, thanking Schrader on the sleeve of his most successful album ever, and offered him this song, which had been tried out with The E.Street Band during the sessions which led up to the 'Born In The USA' album. It became the title of Schrader's 1987 film starring Michael J. Fox and Joan Jett.

This was the song Springsteen used to open the second half of the show on his 1992 tour, and it racks up alongside 'Glory Days' and 'Badlands' as a live favourite. The version here is frenetic and frenzied and comes complete with Bruce's pulpit-bashing sermonising. When it comes to four-on-the-floor, hard pushing rock'n'roll songs, nobody does it better. The real, the only selling point of 'Plugged', is the rampaging workout on 'Light Of Day'. Springsteen's 'Plugged' is the great lost opportunity, bought only by completists: not so much 'Unplugged' as Unplayed.

GREATEST HITS

(COLUMBIA, COL 4785552, RELEASED: FEBRUARY 1995)

"I'd been working on a record of my own for a while, in spurts…" Springsteen told VH-1's Mike Kaufman, **"and I got to a place where I wasn't sure if I was gonna finish it. It didn't quite have the focus that I like my records to have. Jon called me one night and he read off a sequence, the sequence that's on there, and it just seemed like a good idea. We'd never had anything where if you didn't know about what I was doing over the years, you could go into the store and pick up one CD that would give you a broad cross-section of the things I'd been writing about."**

Long-time fans were surprised at the release of a Bruce Springsteen 'Greatest Hits' collection, while cynics noted that the timing coincided with the Grammy Awards ceremony, which featured a heavy Springsteen presence. In the end, he came away clutching four awards for 'Streets Of Philadelphia': Song Of The Year, Best Song Written For A Motion Picture Or Television, Best Rock Song and Best Male Rock Vocal.

Even more of a surprise than the album's actual release were its contents, and the fact that the final four tracks reunited Bruce with the full E.Street Band in the studio for the first time in a decade.

The CD-buying generation had come into its own following the release of 'Born In The USA' in 1984, and Dire Straits' 'Brothers In Arms' the following year. Vinyl albums allowed only 20 minutes comfortably on each side before the sound quality dipped, while Compact Discs had room for nearly 80 minutes' worth of music. Within a decade, CDs became the main source of music for the majority of record buyers.

Record companies weren't slow to reactivate back catalogue material for the burgeoning

Compact Disc market: far too often though, CDs were pressed from third or fourth generation masters, with comparatively poor sound quality. Little effort was made to adapt cover art to the smaller format or to supply contemporaneous bonus tracks or additional sleeve information. On Springsteen's CD sequence, for example, Columbia's largesse didn't extend even to adding the lyrics to 'The Wild, The Innocent & The E.Street Shuffle'.

Led Zeppelin's original CD releases were an industry joke and it wasn't until the Remastered versions hit the market a decade later that the fans got what they deserved. In most cases, having replaced vinyl copies with CD, fans had to fork out again when the titles were re-released some years later with cleaned up, Remastered sound. David Bowie and Elvis Costello, though, received praise for their sequential releases, which boasted bonus tracks, rare photos and comprehensive sleeve notes.

As the back catalogues were endlessly mined and re-released, the obvious format to bring fans back to the record stores in large numbers was the Greatest Hits package. Artists who were perceived to have passed their sell-by date, suddenly found themselves back in chart favour with a Greatest Hits package. Simple Minds' collection outsold even Madonna, Alison Moyet's Singles Collection débuted at No.1, while The Beautiful South held sway over everything – even 'The Beatles At The BBC' – during the latter half of 1994.

With the new-found possibility of squeezing an artist's entire career onto one shiny disc, it really came as no surprise that Bruce Springsteen should crack and enter the market place. He had already supplied the obligatory live album, all that was now missing was a Greatest Hits.

In fact, to help promote Springsteen's 1992 UK shows, Columbia had released a 16-track Greatest Hits collection ('Tougher Than The Rest') for promotional purposes. It is interesting to compare that selection with the official release three years later – on the promo CD, space was also found for 'Atlantic City', 'For You', 'Incident On 57th Street', 'Lucky Town', '57 Channels…' and 'Tougher Than The Rest'.

The official 'Greatest Hits' obviously drew heavily on Springsteen's biggest-selling package – four tracks were drawn from 'Born In The USA' – but nothing was selected from either of his first two albums. Of course, everyone who has ever owned a Bruce Springsteen album has their own idea of how a Greatest Hits album should be compiled, but as with 'Live 1975-85', this one does seem designed to capitalise on the huge success of 'Born In The USA', while ignoring some very strong, pre-1975 material.

A simple strategy to keep everyone happy would have been a limited edition two CD package. Fresh converts would have been happy with all the hits, ensuring a high chart placing, while long-time fans would have been delighted to get the second bonus disc, which could either have been crammed with rare B-sides still unavailable on CD (see 'Odds & Ends' Chapter) or have included some of the "ones that got away": 'This Hard Land', 'Murder Incorporated', 'Frankie', 'The Fever', 'Rendezvous' or any of the dozens more which have been available on bootleg for years.

However, despite its misleading title (only three of the 18 songs had ever cracked the UK Top 10), 'Bruce Springsteen's Greatest Hits' did manage to cover the journey from the freewheeling 'Born To Run' right up to the pensive 'Streets Of Philadelphia'. For *aficionados* though, the real interest lay in the four 'new' tracks which concluded the album: 'Murder Incorporated', 'This Hard Land', 'Blood Brothers' and 'Secret Garden'.

Music aside, Greatest Hits was nicely packaged. It was particularly good to see the 'Bruce Springsteen's Back' photo (originally used to promote 1975's Roxy shows) finally used, and Springsteen's own song-by-song commentary was a revealing bonus.

As it is, the album stands as a landmark for Springsteen. A happy second marriage, the satisfactions of fatherhood and the fact that he is reunited with his band, suggest a continuity and bode well for the future. At the time of writing, Springsteen is even being strongly tipped to tour again with the the E.Street Band. All the more disquieting then to realise that the best of the 'new' songs on this collection were written a decade previously. And while 'Secret Garden' and 'Blood Brothers' were pleasant enough additions, if they were the strongest indications of Springsteen's recorded future, then a pallid time would be had by all.

Springsteen's come a long way from the cocky kid grinning out of Asbury Park. He has given some of his very best in concerts all over the world and has tried hard to capture that empathy and commitment on record. He has come very close to achieving it. While there are serious omissions – and baffling inclusions – Bruce Springsteen Greatest Hits is an indulgent opportunity to appreciate the full power of one of rock'n'roll's true originals.

Springsteen himself told *Guitar World*'s Neil Strauss: "I like the classic idea of hits – it was sort of like 50,000,000 Elvis Fans Can't Be Wrong...The album was supposed to be fun, something that you could vacuum the rug to... I wanted to introduce my music to younger fans, who for 12 bucks could get a pretty good overview of what I've done over the years. And for my older fans I wanted to say 'This still means something to me now, you still mean something to me now'. It was just kind of a way of reaffirming the relationship that I've built up with my audience over the past 25 years, which outside of my family is the most important relationship in my life."

Full track listing: Born To Run (4.30), Thunder Road (4.49), Badlands (4.03), The River (5.00), Hungry Heart (3.21), Atlantic City (3.57), Dancing In The Dark (4.03), Born In The

USA (4.41), My Hometown (4.13), Glory Days (3.49), Brilliant Disguise (4.16), Human Touch (5.10), Better Days (3.45), Streets Of Philadelphia (3.16), Secret Garden (4.28), Murder Incorporated (3.58), Blood Brothers (4.34), This Hard Land (4.52)

STREETS OF PHILADELPHIA

"I was trying to think as cinematically as I could. The idea was to contrast how this person was in a life and death struggle with all these images of life – fire engines, people at the bakery…" Springsteen hadn't even seen a rough cut of the film, but in conversation with director Jonathan Demme, he grasped the mood of Hollywood's first mainstream film to deal with AIDS.

It was the first Springsteen song to be specifically written for a film, rather than just being utilised on the soundtrack. Demme's 1993 film *Philadelphia* won Tom Hanks his first Oscar, and Springsteen his first Oscar for Best Original Song. 'Streets Of Philadelphia' became Springsteen's biggest-ever UK hit single, reaching No.2 in April 1994.

As with the 'Nebraska' album, it was the demo version of this song which finally made it onto the soundtrack, Demme having originally cut the title sequence to Neil Young's 'Southern Man'. Demme told *Mojo*'s Mat Snow: "I wanted someone whose constituency might arguably not be disposed towards a film that explored AIDS… It was not the call to action, anthem rock, blazing guitar, out on the highway kind of thing. It was this extraordinarily intimate song. We laid it on and it was exquisite."

In a dignified acceptance speech at the Oscars, which contrasted strongly with Hanks', Springsteen noted: "You do your best work and you hope that it pulls out the best in your audience… and it takes the edge off fear and allows us to recognise each other through our veil of differences. I always thought that was one of the things popular art was supposed to be about, along with the merchandising and all the other stuff…"

SECRET GARDEN

"I wrote very quickly… it's about the unknowability of people in general… The record I was working on last year touched on that… how difficult it is to know even ourselves."

Originally written for Human Touch, 'Secret Garden' was the first single to be lifted off the album; a brooding, slow ballad, with Clarence Clemons' saxophone well to the fore ("The Big Man sweeter than ever," notes Bruce).

MURDER INCORPORATED

"I wrote it in 1982 when I wrote the 'Nebraska' stuff" Springsteen told Robert Hilburn, "The idea is that murder has been incorporated into the society very systematically, a system that basically has set itself up so that violence is one of its by-products. The whole idea of a constant class of disenfranchised people seems to be accepted as the price of doing business. That's what the song is about, and it's probably more relevant now than when I wrote it." Pounding long-time favourite of fans, *Murder Incorporated* was the title of a 1960 Peter Falk gangster movie.

BLOOD BROTHERS

'Blood Brothers' drew on the reconvening of Springsteen's best loved band after the ill-conceived tour of 1992. In style, similar to the material on 'Lucky Town' and nice to hear Bruce's harmonica playing is as good as ever.

"'Blood Brothers' was about trying to understand the meaning of friendship as you grow older," Springsteen told Neil Strauss. "I guess I wrote it the night before I went into the studio with the band, and I was trying to sort out what I was doing and what those relationships meant to me now, and what those types of friendships mean as a person moves through life."

THIS HARD LAND

Shortlisted for 'Born In The USA' 10 years before, drummer Max Weinberg claimed this as his favourite Bruce Springsteen song. "I guess this kinda sums it up with one of the ones that got away. Cut in the frontier town of NYC in Jan '95 and featuring me and the band and one of my favourite last verses," wrote Bruce.

'This Hard Land' is one of Springsteen's best-ever narratives. A tale of brotherly loyalty, played out against the arid Tex-Mex border, nestling next to the Rio Grande. Another good example of Springsteen's cinematic style of writing, 'This Hard Land' evokes Red River, The Border, The Searchers…

Unfortunately, the re-recorded version included here flattens one of Springsteen's best-ever songs. Originally cut in an acoustic, 'Nebraska'-style, and played to great effect that way during the 1993 tour, the 1995 version is subsumed by cluttered keyboards and saxophone. Simpler is better.

"A pretty tough little song," is how Springsteen described it to Robert Hilburn. "You've always got to feel there is a tomorrow. I want to hold that idea and pass that hope on to my children and my fans and their children…"

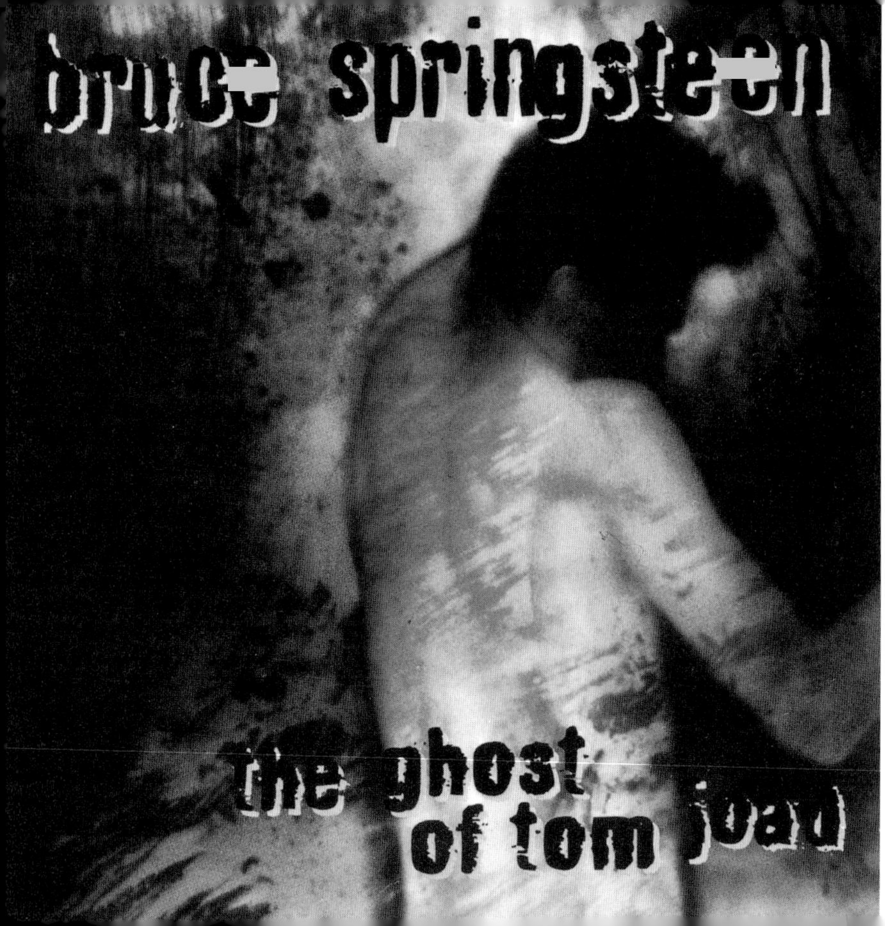
bruce springsteen
the ghost
of tom joad

THE GHOST OF TOM JOAD

(COLUMBIA CD 481650; RELEASED NOVEMBER 1995)

"I think what people are feeling is other people's fingerprints on their minds." Speaking to *Musician* magazine's Neil Strauss late in 1995, Springsteen was characteristically eloquent and reflective. Ironically, talking about 'Bruce Springsteen Greatest Hits' – his most 'packaged' record ever – Springsteen queries: "What are your memories? What are your ideas? Everything is pre-packaged and sold to you as desirable or seductive in some fashion. So how do you find out who you are, create your own world, find your own self? That's the business of rock music in the Nineties."

Encouragingly, in that same interview, Springsteen spoke of his willingness to revisit his past, with an eye to a Box Set ("It might be fun… to throw together some sort of collection of stuff…"). He even admits to wishing that he "hadn't been as rigid as I've been about what I put out… Certainly, I go back and realize that there are many out-takes that should have been released at different times. I still wish I'd put more records out".

Following the release of 'Greatest Hits' in February 1995, Springsteen proved to be spectacularly active. He co-produced, co-wrote and played on Joe Grushecky's 'American Babylon' album. There was something in Grushecky's pumping iron, bar band rock'n'roll which struck a chord in Springsteen, who not only jumped up for a 15 song set with Grushecky's band The Iron City Houserockers, but also went out to actively promote the album, sitting in on interviews with Grushecky.

Springsteen's most prestigious 1995 appearance came at the opening concert for Cleveland's Rock & Roll Hall of Fame in September. Back in tandem with The E. Street Band for their first concert together in seven years, Springsteen played back up for Chuck Berry and Jerry Lee Lewis, then joined Bob Dylan for an emotive duet on 'Forever Young'.

Late in October, Springsteen made his second appearance at a Neil Young Bridge Benefit show. He appeared solo, and two songs from The Ghost of Tom Joad made their live première (the title track and 'Sinaloa Cowboys'). Bruce's eight song set also included 'This Hard Land' and 'Seeds', as well as encores with Young of 'Down By The River' and 'Rocking In The Free World'.

The one show that took everyone by surprise was Springsteen's '1995 European Tour'! For some reason best known to himself, Bruce decided to blitz Berlin. On July 9, he appeared at East Berlin's Cafe Eckstein to play with Wolfgang Niedecken and his Leopardefellband. Ostensibly there to film a video for the live version of 'Hungry Heart', which was to be released as a single later in 1995, Springsteen turned the night into a rock'n'roll celebration, tearing into 'Twist And Shout', 'Honky Tonk Women', 'Glory Days', 'Jumpin' Jack Flash' and 'Highway 61 Revisited'.

With so much activity during the early part of 1995, it looked as though a Bruce

Springsteen album was a certainty for Christmas. The smart money was on a new studio album with The E. Street Band. Following the kiss and make up reconciliation on 'Greatest Hits', long-time Springsteen-watchers were convinced that the first full Bruce and the band album since 'Born In The USA' was on the cards – titles known to have been recorded with the band were 'Father's Day', 'Blind Spot' and 'Between Heaven & Hell'. It was, surely, only a matter of time.

But then, true to form, Springsteen tugged the rug from under everybody's feet, and rush-released the effectively solo 'Ghost Of Tom Joad'. At his specific request, the album was released with the minimum of publicity and hype. It was an audacious move, particularly as in the pre-Christmas rush, Tom Joad was stacked up against new albums from The Beatles, Queen and The Rolling Stones.

'The Ghost Of Tom Joad' is the sound of Bruce Springsteen doing what he does best: telling stories, and drawing the listener into a closed world of his own creation. Since the release of 'Nebraska' – until now Springsteen's most obviously 'folk' statement – the Unplugged phenomenon has made rock fans more tolerant of acoustic music, but the overwhelming bleakness of 'The Ghost Of Tom Joad' still managed to alienate more fans than it enticed.

It is nevertheless a bold record from Springsteen to have made. 'The Ghost Of Tom Joad' saw him put domestic bliss and contented parenthood behind him, take one giant step back, and re-employ himself again as a songwriter, immersing himself in unfamiliar characters and situations.

Much of 'The Ghost of Tom Joad' deals with migrants. But far removed from the American dream of the pioneer spirit taming new frontiers, these are people driven by poverty and desperation from one hopeless home to the next. It is a theme which has fascinated Springsteen since he began performing Ry Cooder's 'Across The Borderline' in concert.

While the instrumentation is muted, with seven out of the 12 tracks featuring Springsteen solo, accompanying himself simply on guitar and keyboards, there is often a Tex-Mex feel to this album, appropriate on a work that focuses so often on that crucial border. Among the musicians who appear on the five remaining tracks are The E. Street Band's Danny Federici and Gary Tallent, and violinist Soosie Tyrell who accompanied Bruce on his 1992 World Tour.

What is warm and inviting about the record, despite the bleak and uncompromising nature of the narratives, is its rough and ready feel. Springsteen sings with real fervour, but sound uncertain, as though the songs have only just been started, and he is unsure just how they'll turn out and resolve themselves. Nowhere is this more apparent than on 'Galveston Bay', where Springsteen gets to play God, and decide which of the two protagonists lives and dies.

Springsteen has always had the ability to juggle the massively commercial with the poignantly personal: 'The River' was followed by 'Nebraska'; 'Born In The USA' by 'Tunnel Of Love' and now 'Greatest Hits' by 'The Ghost Of Tom Joad'.

As rock music becomes more homogenised and marketed, at a time when every record becomes a package, you have to welcome Springsteen's willingness to take risks with a record like this. While there may be elements which don't quite coalesce here, Springsteen's intentions are admirable. There is much to admire on this album about the man who made it.

THE GHOST OF TOM JOAD

A plaintive, lonely harmonica opens Bruce Springsteen's first album of new material since 1992 and a song of the dispossessed and migrants of the Nineties. The characters here aren't born to run, they're limping along, victims of a ruthless government which has lost interest in them.

Tom Joad is the central character of John Steinbeck's Pulitzer Prize-winning novel *The Grapes Of Wrath*, which was first published in 1939. Steinbeck's story concerns a family of Oklahoma farmers ('Okies') who are driven from their farm by soil erosion and the faceless bankers who repossess their property. Loading up their van, they make their way to California, the promised land.

The Grapes Of Wrath is the towering artistic achievement of America's dust bowl depression of the Thirties, and provides fertile territory for Springsteen's most intriguing and off-centre album since 'Nebraska'. Memorably played by Henry Fonda in John Ford's 1940 film, Tom Joad vows: "I'll be all around in the dark. I'll be everywhere… I'll be in the way guys yell when they're mad, and I'll

be in the way kids laugh when they're hungry and they know supper's ready. And when the people are eating the stuff they raise, living in the houses they build – I'll be there too." Sentiments which Springsteen echoes in the third verse of his song.

The film ends with an unforgettable speech from Tom's mother, played by Oscar-winning Jane Darwell: "Rich fellas come up, and they die, and their kids ain't no good, and they die out, but we keep a-comin'. We're the people that live. Can't wipe us out, can't lick us. We'll go on forever, Pa, because we're the people."

John Steinbeck had already influenced Springsteen's writing. 'Adam Raised A Cain' on 1978's 'Darkness On The Edge Of Town' also found its source in a Steinbeck novel, *East Of Eden* – memorable today as the film which in 1955 introduced James Dean to the world.

In 1940, America's premier folk-poet, Woody Guthrie, wrote a song 'Tom Joad', also inspired by Steinbeck's character. Guthrie's was the silent shadow which had stalked Springsteen's 'Nebraska', and it was Woody's anthem 'This Land Is Your Land' which Bruce included on the 'Live 1975-85' box set.

STRAIGHT TIME

As bleak and hopeless as Dylan's 'Ballad of Hollis Brown', in this case too, suicide seems to be the only exit. 'Straight Time' sounds as if it could have walked straight out 'Nebraska' and onto here, with its tale of petty criminals and their reluctance – or inability – to go straight.

HIGHWAY 29

'Highway 29' takes us back to the territory Springsteen stalked on the title track of 'Nebraska', telling of robbery with violence and an emptiness of the heart.

YOUNGSTOWN

The best track here, which kicks in with the album's only really convincing chorus. 'Youngstown' is a brilliantly told tale of successive generations growing up in the iron ore town of the title. It is a wide-ranging story, spanning the Civil War, through World War II, Korea and Vietnam, to the present day. A chilling depiction of a Hell on Earth, which recalls Dylan's 'With God On Our Side' in its sweeping re-telling of American history. Springsteen has never sounded more convincing or more involved in his story than on 'Youngstown'.

SINALOA COWBOYS

Echoes again of Woody Guthrie. This time the similarity is to Guthrie's 'Deportees', which Springsteen performed in concert during the early Eighties. 'Sinaloa Cowboys' is a tale of Mexican immigrants forced into drug manufacture, to compensate for the exploitative labour rates and culminates with the heartbreaking conclusion of a brother's death. While at times, like much of the rest of the album, the song is lyrically cumbersome ("methamphetamine" is not the easiest word to slip into a song) 'Sinaloa Cowboys' stands as Springsteen's best vocal of the album.

THE LINE

Springsteen's troubled fascination with the Mexican-American border is evident across the whole album. The Line is the densely-packed tale of a border guard, whose job is to keep drug smugglers and migrant families out of the United States. The story recalls Jack

Nicholson's 1981 film *The Border*, for which Ry Cooder's heartbreaking 'Across The Borderline' was written. True love doesn't last in 'The Line', and in the best heart-breaking tradition, the narrator spends the rest of his life, gone across the borderline.

BALBOA PARK

On a record which is wilfully light on laughs, this is the album's bleakest and most despairing song. 'Balboa Park' wallows in poverty and low life. Drug running, male prostitution and death are all that's on offer, and even Springsteen seems brought down by his subject matter here.

DRY LIGHTNING

The album's strongest and most affecting love song. A tale of obsession, but the romance becomes stained when you realise the object of the narrator's passion is a hooker. Atmospheric and poignant, 'Dry Lightning' is nonetheless shot through with despair.

THE NEW TIMER

This track boasts the album's best narrative, again drawing strongly on Woody Guthrie's ramblin' yarns of the Thirties and Forties. Springsteen sings in a voice as bleak and chilling as a cold North wind, as he tells of a hobo's murder. The death seems pointless, makes no sense, the result of "somebody killin' just to kill". There is a lovely evocation of life away from hard travelling, as Springsteen sings wistfully of a "small house sittin' trackside/with the glow of the saviour's beautiful light".

ACROSS THE BORDER

Haunting and poignant, deft and heartfelt, the atmosphere is heightened by Springsteen's harmonica and Soosie Tyrell's violin. This track tells again of desperate Mexican migrants, who flock North, hoping for a slice of the American Dream life in the USA.

GALVESTON BAY

A long way away from Glen Campbell's 'Galveston'. Here Springsteen tells of a Vietnamese immigrant who came to the myth-

ical promised land following the Vietcong victory. Inspired by Louis Malle's film *Alamo Bay*, Springsteen contrasts Le Bin Son's story with that of native-born Billy Sutter. 'Galveston Bay' is a deft and scene-setting tale of the conflict between immigrants and those who still want 'America for Americans'. It continues, tensely, with violence, then finds tranquility, as Springsteen sings with an almost Biblical allegory of Billy casting "his nets into the water of Galveston Bay".

MY BEST WAS NEVER GOOD ENOUGH

A deliberate chain necklace of cliché, Springsteen rails against the complacency of Forrest Gump's world view. Those who loved Tom Hanks' 'philosophy' will hate this ("'Stupid is as stupid does' and all the rest of that shit…"). A strange and subdued ending for an album which ranks as one of the most intriguing, but nonetheless baffling, of Bruce's career.

ODDS & ENDS

While most of his energies go into studio albums and tours, over the years Springsteen has built up a substantial collection of B-sides, album rarities and one-off singles which would make up a whole album's worth of material. One imaginative bootlegger did just that with the cheekily titled 'Another Side Of Bruce Springsteen'. Most of it is available on CD, and any difficulties obtaining the songs mentioned here can be rectified by a telephone call to 'Badlands', whose details are on page xiii.

This section is concerned with the best fully-formed songs, covers or performances by Springsteen, which are not contained in his official album releases. These songs and performances are an essential addition to any full understanding and appreciation of Bruce Springsteen.

Springsteen's first live performance on record came with an edited 'Devil With The Blue Dress On' on the 1979 'No Nukes' album (Asylum L62027). Originally recorded by Mitch Ryder & The Detroit Wheels in 1966, 'Devil With The Blue Dress On' had been a regular concert closer of Springsteen's live shows from 1975 onwards. On this album, Springsteen also duets with Jackson Browne on 'Stay' – popularised in Britain by The Hollies.

'In Harmony 2' (CBS 8545110) was a 1981 charity compilation which featured a lively 1975 Springsteen performance of 'Santa Claus Is Comin' To Town', inspired by The Crystals' contribution to Phil Spector's classic 1963 Christmas album. Bruce is full of Yuletide cheer as he asks the band if they've been good, and if Clarence has been practising hard enough for Santa to bring him a new saxophone.

Not as good, but nevertheless equally festive was 'Merry Christmas Baby', which appeared as an additional track on the 12″ single of 'War' in 1986 and on 1987's 'A Very Special Christmas' (A&M 393911-2).

Springsteen contributed to USA For Africa's 'We Are The World' single and his 'Trapped' was the highlight of their 1985 album (Columbia USAIDF1). Springsteen had been beguiled by the Jimmy Cliff song on a cassette he heard, and having rewritten the words, began incorporating it during live concerts between 1981 and 1985. It is a coiled, purposeful rendition, one of The E.Street Band's best-ever live songs, snapping into place during the chorus, following on from Bruce's muted reading of the verses and Roy Bittan's haunting synthesiser line. The performance on the 'USA For Africa' album was taken from a live show at Meadowlands Arena, New Jersey in August 1984.

In 1988, Springsteen contributed two songs to 'Folkways: A Vision Shared, A Tribute To Woody Guthrie & Leadbelly' (Columbia 460905). Bruce chose two of Woody's most political songs, 'I Ain't Got No Home' and 'Vigilante Man', as his contributions. 'I Ain't Got No Home' was written following Guthrie's experience of observing the dispossessed Okies trudging from State to State looking for work during the dust-blown depression of the 1930s. Springsteen immersed himself in Guthrie's life and work during the early '80s, regularly performing 'This Land Is Your Land' in concert, steeping himself in Guthrie's original Folkways recordings from the 1940s, all of which lead up to the recording of 'Nebraska'. 'Vigilante Man' is Guthrie's scornful observation of the realities of mob law and the mentality of the lynch gang. With contributions from U2, Emmylou Harris, John Mellencamp and Bob Dylan, 'Folkways' is one of the few tribute albums to actually hit the mark, the artists involved contributing because they admire the original artist's work, but not afraid to reinterpret it in their own fashion.

British journalist Roy Carr had been moved by the NordoffRobbins charity's efforts to communicate with handicapped children through music. In 1990, Carr put together 'The Last Temptation Of Elvis' (NME CD 038/039), which had the Top Pop Acts of Today (The Pogues, Jesus & Mary Chain, Pop Will Eat Itself) as well as Elvis fans of long-standing (Paul McCartney, Robert Plant, Dion) covering their favourite song from an Elvis movie.

BRUCE SPRINGSTEEN : ODDS & ENDS

Carr, who had met Springsteen in Los Angeles during 1975, was delighted, if a little surprised, to have him on board for the charity album. Springsteen was in the middle of his five-year silence between 'Tunnel Of Love' and 'Human Touch', so his involvement was a signal achievement. Carr was even more surprised at Bruce's choice of cover. He had Bruce pencilled in for either 'Follow That Dream' or 'Can't Help Falling In Love', both of which Springsteen had been regularly performing in concert. As it was, Springsteen submitted a slam-bam three-minute version of 'Viva Las Vegas'.

Another 1990 release was 'The Harry Chapin Tribute' (Relativity 88561-1047-2), which featured Springsteen performing a beautiful version of Chapin's 'Remember When The Music', and delighting the audience with his tales of how the legendarily charity-oriented Chapin kept bugging him to get more involved in social issues and charity work. "I play one night for me," was Chapin's motto, "and one night for the other guy."

For the benefit of completists, Springsteen contributed one line to Steve Van Zandt's Artists Against Apartheid project, 'Sun City' in 1985. He can also be heard singing young Evan James' favourite song 'Chicken Lips & Lizard Hips' on the 1991 'For Our Children' album. And on the 1994 Tribute To Curtis Mayfield album, Springsteen turned in a lacklustre 'Gypsy Woman', appearing alongside all the usual suspects – Rod Stewart, Elton John and Eric Clapton.

Bruce-related releases include 'Cover Me' (Rhino RNIN 70700) – a 1986 compilation of acts who've covered Springsteen songs; all the obvious choices are there: Patti Smith ('Because The Night'), Dave Edmunds ('From Small Things…'), Southside Johnny & The Asbury Jukes ('The Fever'), as well as contributions from The Hollies, Johnny Cash, The Beat Farmers and Robert Gordon.

'Hearts Of Stone' (Epic 82994) is Southside Johnny & The Asbury Jukes' 1978 album, a Springsteen release in all but name. The title track was recorded for 'Darkness On The Edge Of Town', and the Southside version is simply the E.Street band original, with Bruce's vocals lifted off and replaced by Johnny's. Springsteen also contributed the otherwise unavailable 'Talk To Me', as well as co-writing 'Trapped Again'.

While working on 'The River', Springsteen and Miami Steve took time off to supervise Gary 'US' Bonds' 1981 comeback album, 'Dedication' (EMI AML 3017). Bonds' 1961 hit 'Quarter To Three' had been a regular Springsteen concert encore from 1974–1981. As well as overseeing the project, Springsteen also contributed 'This Little Girl' (which helped Bonds' chart comeback), the title track and 'Your Love'. Also including covers of songs by The Beatles and Jackson Browne, 'Dedication' was a triumphant return for Bonds, who had been reduced to singing at McDonald's openings until rescued by Springsteen and Van Zandt.

Unfortunately, the magic couldn't be rekindled for the second collaboration, 1982's 'On The Line' (EMI AML 3022). The highlight was a storming version of 'Rendezvous', which Springsteen had left off 'Darkness On The Edge Of Town', and which in Bonds' hands, became a little touch of Phil Spector in the night. The same can't be said for the remaining six Springsteen compositions on the album. 'Angelyne' just about passes muster, a poor relation of 'From Small Things (Big Things One Day Come)', but – in the days before 'Man's

Job' – 'Out Of Work' and 'Club Soul City' were the most embarrassing songs Springsteen had put his name to.

Springsteen came relatively late to the world of tucking away unreleased songs on the B-sides of singles: the frenetic 'Held Up Without A Gun' coupled 'Hungry Heart' in 1980 while the unremarkable, but nonetheless otherwise unobtainable, 'The Big Payback' was a European-only B-side to 'Open All Night' in 1982.

The fun really started with the plundering of 'Born In The USA' for singles during 1984/85. 'Pink Cadillac' had been intended for the album and subsequently did appear as the B-side of the album's first single, 'Dancing In The Dark'. 'Pink Cadillac' is another of those great Springsteen car songs, centred around a killer riff, with smouldering and sexy lyrics. Natalie Cole took the song to UK No. 5 in 1988.

Tom Waits' 'Jersey Girl' was discussed in its place at the end of Live 1975-85, but it actually first appeared as the B-side to 'Cover Me' in 1984. It's worth noting that Springsteen adds a final verse to the Waits original. The pensive 'Janey, Don't You Lose Heart' appeared on the B-side of 'I'm Goin' Down'.

The real incentive to buy the 12" 'Cover Me' was for 3'52" of 'Shut Out The Light', one of Springsteen's most haunting songs and quite inexplicably consigned to a B-side. The song had begun life during the roll Springsteen found himself on while recording at home for the sessions which became 'Nebraska'. It was shortlisted for 'Born In The USA', but Springsteen felt it didn't sit comfortably on that album; ironic, as its source was the same as that of the album's title track: Ron Kovic's Vietnam memoir, *Born On The 4th Of July.* Bleak and strangely remote, 'Shut Out The Light' is one of Springsteen's finest ever songs about isolation, about a man cut off from his community, his wife and from himself.

The 1985 'I'm On Fire' single, as well as boasting Arthur Baker's 'Freedom Mix' of 'Born In The USA', a lurid, Spectoresque reworking of the song, also had 1'50" of 'Johnny Bye Bye' on the 12". Lifting its opening lines from Chuck Berry's 'Bye Bye Johnny', Springsteen's song was his response to the death of Elvis Presley. Having memorably performed the song virtually solo and to great effect during his 1981 UK tour, when he came to record it, Springsteen unwisely soaked the

song in synthesisers and paced it too fast. In accelerating the song, Springsteen seems to lose the intimacy of the live version, and the 'Johnny Bye Bye' here is a pale shadow of its live incarnation. Nevertheless, in its sly rockabilly version, it is still worth at least hearing.

'Stand On It' appeared on the 12" of 'Glory Days', a slam-bam, don't hold your breath rock'n'roller, with some fabulous boogie-woogie piano playing out the back. A song in the style and spirit of 'Held Up Without A Gun' and 'Light Of Day', and like all great rock-'n'roll songs, it weighs in at under three minutes. Recorded during the lengthy sessions which led up to 'Born In The USA', Springsteen was having fun with the song and performed it regularly live during 1984/85.

'War' was the first single to be lifted off the Live 1975-85 box set in 1986, it featured a 10-minute live version of 'Incident On 57th Street' on the 12", with a scorching guitar solo thrown in for good measure...

In 1987, 'Roulette' appeared on the 12" of 'Tougher Than The Rest'. Recorded in 1979 at 'The River' sessions, it was Springsteen's angry response to the nuclear accident at Three Mile Island earlier that year. Fearsomely

fast drums usher in a tearaway song about a community destroyed by fear of the unknown. It is an impressive performance, but in his haste to convey the threat, Springsteen gabbles his vocals, somewhat diminishing the song's impact.

Over the next few years there would be sporadic non-album releases ('Part Man, Part Monkey', 'Thirty Days Out', 'Lucky Man', 'Two For The Road'), but the best of the bunch was a 25-minute 12″ EP, 'Chimes Of Freedom' (Columbia 4C44445) released in June 1988. As well as a big stadium version of 'Tougher Than The Rest' from 'Tunnel Of Love', the four-track EP also featured a pounding live rocker, 'Be True', which had appeared as a B-side to the European single of 'Sherry Darling', and on 'Fade Away' in the USA. 'Born To Run' appears as a haunting solo reflection, barely recognisable as the quintessential high-octane rocker which had fuelled Springsteen's reputation during the 1970s.

Springsteen had become enamoured again of his best-known song, and introducing the solo, acoustic 'Born To Run' during his 1988 Tunnel Of Love tour, he announced rather touchingly: "I wrote this song when I was 24 years old, sitting on the end of my bed in Long Branch, New Jersey and thinking 'Here I come, world'… When I wrote it, I guess I figured it was a song about a guy and a girl who wanted to run and kept on running… But as I got older, and as I sang it over the years, it sort of opened up, and I guess I realized that it was about two people out searching for something better. Searching for a place they could stand and try and make a life for themselves. And I guess in the end they were searching for home, something that I guess everybody looks for all their lives. I've spent my life looking for it. Anyway this song has kept me good company on my search. I hope it's kept you good company on your search."

Ironically, it is on a cover version that you get Springsteen *in excelsis*. Recorded in Stockholm on July 3, 1988, Springsteen prefaces the song by announcing: "Earlier today Amnesty International announced a worldwide tour to celebrate the… Declaration of Human Rights. The Declaration of Human Rights is a document that was signed by every government in the world 40 years ago, recognising the existence of certain inalienable human rights for everyone, regardless of your race, sex, colour, your political opinion or the type of government you live under. I was proud to have been asked and I'm proud to participate... So I'd like to dedicate this next song to the people of Amnesty International, and their idea. So when we come to your town, come on out, support the tour, support Human Rights for everyone now. And let freedom ring."

And he leads The E.Street Band into a blinding, overwhelming version of Bob Dylan's anthemic 'Chimes Of Freedom'. Dylan recorded the song on his transitional 1964 album 'Another Side Of Bob Dylan', it was a song which linked the old Dylan of folk protest with the new poet pursuing a confused and confusing personal odyssey. In Springsteen's hands though, 'Chimes Of Freedom' becomes a clarion call, a ringing anthem, which elevates Dylan's muted solo original into an ensemble piece, a big band version which in no way diminishes the impact of Dylan's extraordinary lyrics.

'Chimes Of Freedom' is one of the best-ever Dylan covers, and certainly one of Springsteen's most fervent performances. It's a performance which fuses the old idealism of the Sixties with a tougher political reappraisal of the late Eighties, all brought together by the man who had begun his career as a "new Dylan" and had swiftly gone on to eclipse his old mentor, before the two drew back level in the Nineties.

'Chimes Of Freedom' is a high point on which to end. The idealism and optimism, the "starry-eyed and laughing" feeling which Dylan captures in the song, is reinforced by Springsteen. He was a late convert to the idea of welding rock'n'roll to political commitment. But once he found that link, Springsteen made it almost better than anyone. Throughout his best work, on record and in performance, Springsteen has come to symbolise an integrity and commitment which many felt had gone adrift in the increasingly corporate and homogenised world which had come to represent rock'n'roll.

Listen to Springsteen tackle 'Chimes Of Freedom' that night in Stockholm, and remind yourself of the power that he could harness, the commitment and care that he could bring to bear. And remind yourself of the words he spoke in another place, at another time, that "In the end, nobody wins unless everybody wins."

INDEX

4TH OF JULY, ASBURY PARK (SANDY) 12
57 CHANNELS (AND NOTHIN' ON) 89
ACROSS THE BORDER.............115
ADAM RAISED A CAIN 29
AIN'T GOT YOU 78
ALL OR NOTHIN' AT ALL 90
ALL THAT HEAVEN WILL ALLOW 79
ANGEL, THE 6
ATLANTIC CITY.............51
BACKSTREETS 21
BADLANDS 28
BALBOA PARK 114
BECAUSE THE NIGHT 71
BETTER DAYS.............92
BIG MUDDY, THE 94
BLINDED BY THE LIGHT 4
BLOOD BROTHERS.............107
BOBBY JEAN 63
BOOK OF DREAMS.............95
BORN IN THE USA 61
BORN TO RUN.............22
BRILLIANT DISGUISE 80
CADILLAC RANCH 40
CANDY'S ROOM 30

CAUTIOUS MAN.............79
CHIMES OF FREEDOM.............125
COVER ME 62
CROSS MY HEART 89
CRUSH ON YOU.............39
DANCING IN THE DARK 63
DARKNESS ON THE EDGE OF TOWN 31
DARLINGTON COUNTY 62
DEVIL WITH THE BLUE DRESS ON 117
DOES THIS BUS STOP AT 82ND STREET? 5
DOWNBOUND TRAIN 62
DRIVE ALL NIGHT.............43
DRY LIGHTNING 114
E. STREET SHUFFLE, THE 12
FACTORY 30
FADE AWAY 41
FIRE 71
FOR YOU 6
GALVESTON BAY 115
GHOST OF TOM JOAD, THE 112
GLORIA'S EYES 89
GLORY DAYS.............63
GROWIN' UP.............4
HIGHWAY 29 113

HIGHWAY PATROLMAN 53
HUMAN TOUCH 88
HUNGRY HEART 39
I AIN'T GOT NO HOME 118
I WANNA MARRY YOU 40
I WISH I WERE BLIND 91
I'M A ROCKER 41
I'M GOIN' DOWN 63
I'M ON FIRE 62
IF I SHOULD FALL BEHIND 93
INCIDENT ON 57TH STREET 13
INDEPENDENCE DAY 38
IT'S HARD TO BE A SAINT IN THE CITY 7
JACKSON CAGE...37
JERSEY GIRL 73
JOHNNY 99 53
JOHNNY BYE BYE...122
JUNGLELAND 23
KITTY'S BACK 13
LEAP OF FAITH 93
LIGHT OF DAY 99
LINE, THE 114
LIVING PROOF..94
LOCAL HERO..93
LONG GOODBYE, THE.....................................92
LOST IN THE FLOOD 5
LUCKY TOWN 93

MAN'S JOB...90
MANSION ON THE HILL 53
MARY QUEEN OF ARKANSAS 5
MEETING ACROSS THE RIVER 23
MERRY CHRISTMAS BABY 117
MURDER INCORPORATED 106
MY BEAUTIFUL REWARD 95
MY BEST WAS NEVER GOOD ENOUGH 115
MY FATHER'S HOUSE 55
MY HOMETOWN 64
NEBRASKA 51
NEW TIMER, THE 115
NEW YORK CITY SERENADE 14
NIGHT 21
NO SURRENDER 63
ONE STEP UP 81
OPEN ALL NIGHT 54
OUT IN THE STREET 39
PARADISE BY THE 'C' 70
POINT BLANK 41
PONY BOY 92
PRICE YOU PAY, THE 43
PROMISED LAND, THE 30
PROVE IT ALL NIGHT 31
RACING IN THE STREET 30
RAISE YOUR HAND 71
RAMROD 42

REAL MAN 92

REAL WORLD 90

REASON TO BELIEVE 55

RED HEADED WOMAN 99

REMEMBER WHEN THE MUSIC 119

RIVER, THE 40

ROLL OF THE DICE 90

ROSALITA (COME OUT TONIGHT) 14

ROULETTE...122

SANTA CLAUS IS COMIN' TO TOWN 117

SECRET GARDEN 105

SEEDS 73

SHE'S THE ONE 23

SHERRY DARLING..37

SHUT OUT THE LIGHT 122

SINALOA COWBOYS...................................114

SOMETHING IN THE NIGHT.........................30

SOUL DRIVER 89

SOULS OF THE DEPARTED 95

SPARE PARTS 79

SPIRIT IN THE NIGHT 6

STAND ON IT...122

STATE TROOPER...54

STOLEN CAR 42

STRAIGHT TIME 113

STREETS OF FIRE 31

STREETS OF PHILADELPHIA 105

TENTH AVENUE FREEZE-OUT 21

THIS HARD LAND 107

THIS LAND IS YOUR LAND 72

THUNDER ROAD 20

TIES THAT BIND, THE....................................36

TOUGHER THAN THE REST 78

TRAPPED 118

TUNNEL OF LOVE.......................................80

TWO FACES 80

TWO HEARTS..38

USED CARS...54

VALENTINE'S DAY..81

VIGILANTE MAN 118

WALK LIKE A MAN 80

WAR 73

WHEN YOU'RE ALONE 81

WILD BILLY'S CIRCUS STORY 13

WITH EVERY WISH 89

WORKING ON THE HIGHWAY 62

WRECK ON THE HIGHWAY 43

YOU CAN LOOK (BUT YOU'D BETTER
    NOT TOUCH)..39

YOUNGSTOWN 113